Pragmatic Meditations on
Learning Community Pedagogy

Other Notable Gordian Knot Books

Putting Universal Human Rights to Work: Policy Actions in the Struggle for Social Justice, by Archibald Stuart, PhD

Malthus, Darwin, Durkheim, Marx, Weber, Ibn Khaldûn: On Human Species Survival, by Walter L. Wallace, PhD

Seminal Sociological Writings: From Auguste Comte to Max Weber: An Anthology of Groundbreaking Works that Created the Science of Sociology, edited by Richard Altschuler, PhD

Seminal Sociological Writings, Vol. 2: From Harriet Martineau to W. E. B. Du Bois: An Anthology of Groundbreaking Works that Created the Science of Sociology, edited by Richard Altschuler, PhD

On the Cutting Edge: Tales of a Cold War Engineer at the Dawn of the Nuclear, Guided Missile, Computer, and Space Ages, by Robert Brodsky, PhD

Women, Marriage, and Wealth, by Joyce A. Joyce, PhD

Where Are We Going? by Miriam Finder Tasini, MD

Reflections on Medicine: Essays by Robert U. Massey, MD, edited by Martin Duke, MD

Contemplative Aging: A Way of Being in Later Life, by Edmund Sherman, PhD

Law and Society, by Stanford M. Lyman, PhD

On Being a Woman Surgeon: Sixty Women Share Their Stories, edited by Preeti R. John, MD

Doctor, Why Does My Face Still Ache? Getting Relief from Persistent Jaw, Ear, and Headache Pain, by Donald R. Tanenbaum, DDS, and S. L. Roistacher, DDS

Dancing on the Tails of the Bell Curve: Readings on the Joy and Power of Statistics, edited by Richard Altschuler, PhD

Identifying and Recovering from Psychological Trauma: A Psychiatrist's Guide for Victims of Childhood Abuse, Spousal Battery, and Political Terrorism, by Brian Trappler, MD

Studies in Structural Sociology, by Frank W. Young, PhD

Pragmatic Meditations on Learning Community Pedagogy

by

Andrew J. Weigert

Gordian Knot Books
An Imprint of Richard Altschuler & Associates, Inc.

Los Angeles

Distributed by Ingram

Pragmatic Meditations on Learning Community Pedagogy. Copyright © 2015 by Andrew J. Weigert. For information contact the publisher, Richard Altschuler & Associates, Inc., at 10390 Wilshire Boulevard, Los Angeles, CA 90024, (424) 279-9118, or send an email to Richard.Altschuler@gmail.com.

Library of Congress Control Number: 2015953085
CIP data for this book are available from the Library of Congress

ISBN-13: 978-1-884092-24-4

Gordian Knot Books is an imprint of
Richard Altschuler & Associates, Inc.

All rights reserved. Except as allowed for fair use, no part of this publication may be reproduced, stored in a retrieval system, or transmitted in any form or by any means, electronic, mechanical, photocopying, recording, or otherwise, without the prior written permission of Richard Altschuler & Associates, Inc.

Printed in the United States of America

Distributed by Ingram

Contents

Preface		vii
Introduction	My Self-Understandings that Inform Learning Community Pedagogy	1
Meditation I	Framework for a Learning Community Pedagogy	8
Meditation II	Teaching Derives from Learning Community Pedagogy	10
Meditation III	Memories of Pedagogical Experiences	12
Meditation IV	Growing a Learning Community	16
Meditation V	Learning Community Emerges from Shared Understandings	23
Meditation VI	Formatting a Learning Community Pedagogy	31
Meditation VII	What May a Learning Community Professor Profess?	37
Meditation VIII	This-Worldly Hope Informs Learning Community Pedagogy	42
Meditation IX	Learning about Teaching in a Learning Community	47
Meditation X	Pedagogical Reversals in a Learning Community	52
Meditation XI	Learning Community Pedagogy and Temporary Answers	63
Meditation XII	Learning Community Characteristics	67
Meditation XIII	Unlearning Conventions To Unleash a Learning Community	73
Meditation XIV	Rethinking Grading Practices for a Learning Community	77
Meditation XV	LCP Within a Religiously Identified University	81
Meditation XVI	Learning as an Evolutionary Community Process	82

Meditation XVII	Intergenerational Learning Communities and a Sense of History	88
Meditation XVIII	Learning Community as Source and Context of Pedagogy	90
Meditation XIX	Why Do Learning Communities Gather at the Circle?	98
Meditation XX	Authenticity and Presence in a Learning Community	101
Meditation XXI	Learning Communities Are Naturally Intellectual	106
Meditation XXII	Classical Foundation Stones of Learning Community Pedagogy	108
Meditation XXIII	How to Spend Learning Time When Community Gathers	112
Meditation XXIV	Personalized Learning Community Reflections on Professor, Student, and Higher Education System	115
Meditation XXV	Premise, Goals, Means, Principle Informing Learning Community	121
Meditation XXVI	Learning Community Works Best in Safe Space and Time	126
Meditation XXVII	Learning and Values in a Learning Community	129
Meditation XXVIII	Some Learning Community Student Responses	131
Meditation XXIX	Innocence versus Seeing in a Learning Community	136
Meditation XXX	Historical Ruptures Illuminate Learning Community Pedagogy	139
Meditation XXXI	Pessimism, Optimism, and Realism in a Learning Community	145
Meditation XXXII	Learning Community Pedagogy Looks toward Social Hope	147
Coda	Reversal of Efficacious Knowledge in a Learning Community: From Pedagogy to Gerogogy	149

Preface

Thanks to the myriad students who shared my journey as a practicing teacher. The first leg of the journey was teaching Sunday school to youngsters, as I began a pilgrimage as a Jesuit. Later, after finishing a Licentiate in Philosophy and an MA in economics at St. Louis University, a late summer reassignment sent me to Colegio San Ignacio in Rio Piedras, Puerto Rico, to learn Spanish and to teach English, algebra, and geometry in English, while helping as an assistant coach (and learning volleyball). The Puerto Rican experience finished with a summer of teaching geometry in Spanish to recent Cuban refugee seminarians, at a Seminary in Aibonito. Next came three years of theological studies at Woodstock College, Maryland. During both philosophy and theology programs, I studied and discussed with small groups of friends—precursors of Learning Community Pedagogy (LCP).

After leaving the Jesuits and receiving a Ph.D. in sociology at the University of Minnesota, I joined the faculty at the University of Notre Dame. LCP emerged over forty-seven years of teaching sociology and required humanities courses at Notre Dame, and one year as a visiting professor at Yale Divinity School. The emergent feature of LCP is understanding a class as a community. My spouse, Kathleen Maas Weigert, already incorporated experiential and community-based learning into her love of teaching. She encouraged me to develop the community dynamic, which I continue to seek.

Finally, another type of "teaching" and "learning" occurs among parents and children: I am grateful for the wonderful teaching and learning that occur with Karen and Sheila every day, and now with son-in-law, Ernie, and granddaughter, seven-year-old Kate.

Introduction:
My Self-Understandings that Inform Learning Community Pedagogy

As this book is about Learning Community Pedagogy (LCP)—or a community learning dynamic that empowers "students" to become effective participants in participatory democratic dynamics—I feel it is important to first inform the reader, in these introductory remarks, of my self-understandings that compose the basis of my arguments in the ensuing "Meditations" on LCP that compose this book.

For me, what we typically take as epistemological components and processes—intellect, concepts, learning—are socially realized and evolutionarily channeled, even if *ex post factum* tools for living. I take a basic pragmatic perspective that is efficacious, therefore, whether it is true or not in any other sense, and enables the human species to survive intergenerationally. My basic epistemological stance, however, never releases from the residual scholasticism that grounds *philosophia perennis*. Labels such as "existential scholasticism" flip-flopped with "scholastic pragmatism" would, perhaps, serve descriptively to reference the kind of perspective that informs my "Meditations" on LCP presented in this book.

Specifically, *existential scholasticism* tries to grasp a perspective that lives at the tense dialectic between, on the one hand, a commitment to empiricism—in the broad sense, as the only public grounding for knowledge—and, on the other hand, to faith in reason and conceptual development. Both of these epistemological values were part of the influences that shaped my perspective: a Jesuit course of training grounded in the neoscholasticism that some of us took as emerging from a commitment to the primacy of "*esse over essentia*"—existence over concept—as discussed by Jacques Maritain and Etienne Gilson. *Scholastic pragmatism* emerged during my graduate sociological studies, from interactionist social-psychology based on the American pragmatism of George H. Mead and his followers at the University of Chicago, and to self study and appreciation of the social phenomenology of Alfred Schutz, as codified in a sociology of knowledge schema of Peter Berger and Thomas Luckmann.

At another level of practical cognition, the perspective shaping my worldview is itself informed by a set of values, in the rather neutral sense of images of informing futures that provide meaning and motive to one's existential perspectives and commitments.

I struggle to remain committed to the following assessments of human species being in its current context. First, humans face a set of critical developments that are unique to our history, namely, anthropogenic global environmental changes—some of which threaten significant and, in part, temporally and causally unpredictable or controllable outcomes—and internationally and terroristically-driven violence with available and, likely, inevitably used weapons of mass destruction—a new threat that passes euphemistically as "WMDs." My sense of crisis originally dawned from a reading of Jose Ortega y Gasset and his cultural analyses of current developments. He followed his understandings of the world, as he saw it to be, with the academic and magisterial imperative for the universities to "rise to the level of the times" and address the critical issues with the intellectual and moral capacities that universities foster.

In today's world, we face another issue not addressed in these meditations on pedagogy or education, that is, the increasing cooptation of universities into the capitalist logic and decision making of ever more expansion, status climbing, and masked profit-making, in terms of payoffs and power points. Ortega y Gasset's writings combine the interpretive play of phenomenology with a powerfully moral commitment to a future that resounds with a pragmatic purpose. The future belongs to the "alert" person who struggles ceaselessly for relevance, that is, for shared understandings of common issues that lead to reconstructions of self and society in the service of a sharable future.

In addition to the above, I build my perspective about LCP on faith in intellect and the public potentiality of shared meanings and empirically-based descriptions of the world as the nest of human species survival. Intellect is the handmaiden of goodness—a handmaiden who uses reason in a wide and historically contingent sense, to generate descriptions of and data about a world that includes everyone's good and everyone's future.

Acquaintance with pragmatism applied to human situations and societies reenforced my commitment to empirically-grounded intellectual efforts. Contemporary dynamics generates a world that seen through the generic lens of "globalization" highlights remaining divisions of ideology, religion, identity, and survival. The socio-economic-cultural dynamics are, therefore, at once unitive and divisive. The dialectic of both unifying and exclusivist dynamics come to a head in the minds of totally committed fighters for both sides, whether in nation-state violence or suicidal, secret-network violence. In a word, intellect fails to function at the heart of this divide. Globally shared interests and values struggle with exclusivist interests and values. Pluralism looks to violence to survive even as global forces look to violence for protection.

Enter intellect: It demands that grounded pluralism and advancing globalization each begin with a best available empirical description of the world as it is. Each worldview, of course, will nuance the description differently, but the search for core understandings of the human situation demands commitment to a shared empirical and intellectual description. The growing banks of data and relevant frameworks provide a basis for such descriptions as well as the probabilities for workable consensus, even among exclusivist worldviews.

LCP builds on the assumption that pluralistic views of the world and our circumstances within it are not sharable if they are ideologically or totally derived from the past, especially a mythical past. We must always remember that the differences that divide us today and threaten each of our futures, especially our common future, are derived from the past—that is, the past remembered as "our past," which does not include those others who are different from us. And how do we know that present others are different from us? The insurmountable answer is that they do not share "our past."

Futures derived from mythical pasts cannot serve as efficacious and sharable cognitive frameworks for a future in which all of us may learn to live in pursuit of our and others' universal values. The very reality of "our past" negates any notion of future sharing of universal values that bestow rights of survival and life-chances on all of us together, which the opening words of "The Universal Declaration of Human Rights" asserts as the basis for a global sense of living humanly and humanely.

LCP builds on the idea that only an ecological and global set of pragmatic arrangements for economic, social, political, educational, spiritual, and psychological institutions can ground all the "our pasts" that divide humans in a way that may (there is no certainty) provide shared understandings, emotions, and activities that may (again there is no certainty) provide a livable future for all of us. At this moment of transcending all "our pasts," we all become, in the best sense of the word and philosophical tradition, hopeful pragmatists willing to put aside *apriori* ideologies and inherited certainties, in such a way as to make it possible to put "our pasts" in the service of "our futures."

LCP thematizes and builds on images of possible shared futures as the operative cognitive and value orientation. Our Pasts survive to inform Our Presents but not at the expense of Our Futures: Pasts and presents enact our differences. These differences survive to vivify our lives but not to threaten our survival. LCP is a pragmatic generalization of the ethnically or ideologically restricted inclusiveness conditionally claimed by past-oriented narratives of the great universalizing religions of the world. The universality of the great religions needs to be translated into this-worldly terms and applied to shared this-worldly tasks and mutual recognition of an emerging shared Earth as our shared future.

In brief, LCP liberates learners through the dynamisms unleashed by the following assumptions:

1. The present world is in a state of profound crisis, that is, at a juncture that requires critical thinking that informs decisions critical for human survival in freedom and dignity;

2. Humans must place their primary faith in intellect as an evolutionary capacity that is socially circumscribed yet potentially universal when liberated from Our Pasts;

3. Intellect is the primary path toward imagining and conceptualizing futures, and the intellectual crisis is to fashion a future that all can see as Our Future;

4. Therefore, LCP focuses on empowering the young to describe their world to themselves and others; to have faith in the intellectual possibilities of all humans; and to reference their world to a sharable global future—Our Future. In a word, students are to become cosmopolitan selves.

Now it is up to the learners to make the world as they would have it be for all. So their active participation and engagement, both cognitively and affectively, is crucial for this ingredient of every contemporary person's worldview.

The outcomes of LCP, then, include realizations based on individual, community, and epistemological dynamics. At the level of the individual, LCP elicits empowerment within a context of shared learning and problem solving, through the application of critical intelligence over ideology or other *aprioris* from Our Past. Within domains of group awareness arise shared understandings informed by an inclusivist dynamic that leads learners to pursue universal values, such as sustaining earthly life-support systems of air, water, soil, and energy; identities based on our common evolutionary and experiential origins and aspirations; and recognition of the importance for all involved to work toward efficacious knowledge, rooted in the realization that only learning that leads to cooperative actions based on shared universal values relevant to critical common issues can fashion shared futures.

These schematic outcomes are themselves manifestations of potentially shared social hope. Social hope based on universal values and the pursuit of efficacious knowledge creates a pragmatic openness toward unknown futures, on the basis of both shared secular faith in empirical knowledge relevant to common issues and mutual love for relevant learning and each other, appropriate to Learning Communities committed to addressing critical and ever-recurring common issues. Note that social hope goes beyond the utilitarian virtue of optimism. Indeed, hope often enters when optimism fails to arise. Optimism, in its barest terms, is a psychological response to means-end rationality: If I believe that this act is a means to achieve that goal, then it follows that I subjectively infuse the means with some putative objectivity of succeeding, that is, I am optimistic about gaining my goal through this means. Yet there are calls to shared action for critical issues that may not carry sure means-end rationality. Enter hope, that is, a commitment to human values that infuses even unlikely actions with an aura of possible futures, and, in some critical junctures, the dynamic of hope carries the day, as social analysts have noted about small committed groups and social movements.

Thus, we come again to this lemma: eloquence that expresses critical intelligence in the service of universal human values, as a charge and mission addressed to all who wish to sustain species being here and now and into possible futures.

Meditation I: Framework for a Learning Community Pedagogy

In brief, here is the framework within which **this version** of a Learning Community Pedagogy arises.

The current situation of the socio-cultural and material dynamics of the world, including human species sustainability and identity, is in crisis. I use "crisis" primarily in the classical sense of a "critical juncture" requiring critical or decisive thinking, decision making, and cooperative action. This classical sense arises from the meaning of the Greek origin of "crisis," that is, *krinein*, to judge critically. From this call to make informed judgments at significant junctures emerges the widespread and folk understanding of "crisis" in ordinary English usage, namely, a situation fraught with heavy consequences that, if not addressed efficaciously, will unleash deeply negative outcomes for those involved.

The contemporary context, furthermore, adds a telling scope to the need to think and act critically: Today's crisis is global; all humans, whether they are aware of it or not, are participants, and the implications concern species being and survival. And as is the case with all social outcomes, the state of crisis is empirically distributed as myriad crises defined and experienced according to an individual's social location. Rising ocean levels, for example, generate a series of empirical crises for both lowland coastal dwellers and higher-elevated inland dwellers, which are mirrored as differential crises for impoverished Third World pedestrians compared to wealthier First World mobile populations. Social location, therefore, is a key feature that generates the probabilities of different passages through the local crises generated by the global crisis dynamic.

The mechanism for realizing these critical passages is intelligence understood socially. Learning Community Pedagogy (LCP) posits intelligence as the universal, evolutionary capacity of humans both to solve problems in the short term and to address issues in the long run. As an evolutionarily selected capacity that is environmentally and circumstantially activated and applied, intelligence precedes culturally and socially reduced types of intellect, such as means-end rationality, value-focused ideology, and nonempirically-referenced faith. The locus of intelligence is in community, with reference to emerging futures that specify a type and process of intelligence.

So we start with the realization that past manifestation of individual and social intelligence generated the current age of crisis, and this realization generates another crisis: Past ways of thinking that generated the crisis are not going to enable humans to pass through the crisis. From this realization arises the pragmatic shift to new and shared imaginings of viable futures; and from these imaginings and our shared intelligence, humans may cooperate to act in new practices that sustain peace, justice, and viable natural and material environments. Thus, we find the need for "crowd intelligence" as more thinkers address shared issues. This move reverses the logic of "forecasting— by extrapolating from "past thinking" or "business as usual"—and generates a dynamic involving the pragmatic move of "backcasting"—from imagined viable and preferable futures. In contrast to "forecasting" from actual conditions, contemporaries need to learn how to "backcast" from more just and sustainable imagined futures, in order to give those futures a probability of realization.

Meditation II: Teaching Derives from Learning Community Pedagogy

Teaching is an odd truncation of the process of shared interaction between or among people. Pedagogy encompasses the entire process of mutual learning and, thus, of mutual teaching. The meaning of acts of teaching abstracted from the interaction of mutual learning derives from the responses of the supposed learner, or complementary other, in this case. The teacher can perform teaching until she or he is blue in the face, but proof of the performance is in the responses of student others, the learners. In a word, if nothing is learned, nothing is taught. Teaching is not solipsistic, miming, or mere performance complete in itself. It is a labeled and abstracted moment in the process of pedagogy. The learner makes the other into a teacher. There can be learning without teaching, but there cannot be teaching without learning.

Learning, in the sense used here, involves participation within a kind of community, a Learning Community (LC). This participation includes students as both learners and teachers and teachers as both learners and teachers. Pedagogy is a way of living, but institutionally separated from the lives of learners; hence the danger of institutionalizing "learning" in empirically separated schools and built environments apart from the daily lives of students.

It is likely that students have little institutional experience with pedagogy in this type of Learning Community. Indeed, formation of such a community within educational establishments is part of the dynamic of teaching-learning for all—their shared pedagogy, whether institutionally supported or not.

What follows are mediations on the processes experienced in a Learning Community Pedagogy, which is one type among the many types and processes of pedagogy.

Meditation III: Memories of Pedagogical Experiences

I offer these meditative memories of learning experience that make up my biography as simply that: reminiscences and meditations. I am not a scholar of educational history or philosophy, so the frame for interpreting what I write in these Meditations is that of an older learner recalling earlier learning moments, and, of necessity, retrospectively interpreting them, since I have no notes or accounts from these biographical time frames.

Long have I wondered about Socrates' claim to accept the Delphic Oracles' naming him the wisest of Athenians. Whether it was a result of gas fumes or preternatural or political sources, the judgment launched an inquiry that reverberates still in the continuing quest for relevant and authentic learning.

Indeed, Socrates resolved his puzzlement through the process of cross-examining social types such as statesmen, poets, craftsmen—all males during that time—whom Athenians presumed would know what it meant to be authentic and virtuous humans. What he discovered, as reported by Plato in the *Apology*, is that these respected personas thought they knew the answers to what it meant to be virtuously human, but they, in fact, did not. In the face of cross-examination, these high status personas did not understand what it was or how to be virtuous. Socrates thus concluded that the Oracle was correct to identify him as the wisest, but the difference between him and other Athenians was simply that, although Socrates did not know the answers either, he was superior only in this seemingly trivial difference: He knew that he did not know! What an astounding paradox: A major exemplar of examined reasonableness, and an extoller of a life lived in endless pursuit of virtue, is validated by his rejection of certitude and any *apriori* or utilitarian claims to a virtuous life immune from critical examination. Hence, it necessarily follows that the unexamined life is not worth living. An unexamined life is that of a robot or fanatic or angel, not of an authentic human seeking to live virtuously.

In my own educational unfolding, I find further paradoxes worthy of informing LCP. Ironically, Plato gave us the text for Socrates' *Apology*. That same Plato, to my recollection, approved the warning above the entryway to his teaching space that said, "Let no one ignorant of mathematics enter here." My distant memory recalls the operative word to be "*ageometrikos*," which strikes my nonprofessional Greek ear as more akin to "ignorant of geometry"—the measurement of spatial arrangements and boundaries that developed into a deductive study of shapes and sizes and their manipulations and relationships. This is the same *apriori* formal approach to teaching/learning that led Plato to ban poets from the Republic, even as he recognized that we humans merely see shadows on the walls of our darkened cave, until we beam the light of the forms and rationality onto the world. The Platonic approach to teaching/learning, it seems to me, informs conventional institutionalized schooling; it is an approach that LCP helps us both to appreciate and go beyond, or, more paradoxically, to go "behind," and reclaim Socrates' cross-examination as members of a community seeking to live, and enable others to live, virtuously.

Enter my reminiscence of a kernel or two from Aristotle. First is Aristotle's dictum that all learning begins in "wonder." Accepting this dictum, I eventually realized that the first move of the professor is to elicit wonder from the students. For most of my career, I began a course, and each class in the course, with the query, "Any questions?" Of course, students very rarely had any questions for a variety of good and bad reasons: from take no risks by asking to never be current with the readings to never side with the professor. At long last, however, I tried to begin by planting seeds that may grow into wonder or present anomalies that may evoke wonder from students; then their internal wonder may drive the motor of learning.

Second, Aristotle insisted that humans are by nature social, or etymologically "political," that is, all humans are born into an ongoing society, which for him meant a built residential community, a "polis" or proto "city." Pedagogy, therefore, is also in and of the polis, of the community, even communities to which students know themselves as members. A Learning Community hopefully emerges within the institutionalized built classroom as a generator of student learning.

Through it all, I gained a sense from Aristotle that learning is thoroughly "natural" to humans, who possess an intrinsic entelechy, or appetite for truth, that motivates them to learn continuously, since there is no end at which the truth is possessed beyond the reach of yet another question or discovery or wonder or obstacle or need to act here and now. His was a dynamic world, in contrast with the view of a Platonic world of fixed forms as the existential circumstances of the human animal. Furthermore, learning is a more than cognitive grasping; it is a form of practical living that addresses problems from the most trivial to the most wide-reaching and powerful—from gardening to polluting to cloning. In a word, learning involves "praxis," or intelligently guided doing. In accord with relevant traditions, from Marxists to pragmatists, an idea is an applicable tool for making a sustainable world.

As a result of my recollections of Aristotelian dicta, I insist with students that learning is a fulfilling and, indeed, pleasurable natural process, albeit a process that becomes stressful, painful, and artificial as a result of societal and institutional transformations of learning into grading, occupational training, status-seeking, risks of social failure, and, thus, threats to self- esteem and self-worth. My borrowings from Aristotle led me to see these negative concomitants as extrinsic to and, at the extreme, corrosive of the natural joy of learning.

Meditation IV: Growing a Learning Community

Learning Community emerges in processes of community formation. In its barest etymological metaphor, a community is a group of interacting persons ("com") who share common walls ("munity"), and are, therefore, present to each other and separated from outsiders. For the time they are together, they share common space, time, focus, preparation, means, and goals. These are more or less structural aspects of their temporarily shared fate. The structural aspects come to life as they channel and elicit the formation of the subjectively shared culture of values and destinies and the instrumental norms to work together toward those goods.

Teacher and students come together, then, and willy nilly engage in interaction that, in itself, generates a culture of their group, their "class," their shared lives, during the structured ephemerality of their gatherings and dispersings. Why does each of them commit to such an experience? What keeps each of them returning and, if they do not, what motivates them to "drop" the course?

Indeed, the enveloping bureaucratic institution makes it more or less difficult to discontinue membership in the "class," sometimes through punitive measures. Such structures of punishment militate against the emergence of a community culture by the group; but such structures seem accepted by most students and faculty, in my experience, as much as the subpar air they breathe in this area.

For clarification, compare a Learning Community with other types of communities: A Learning Community is not a civic community, a recreational community, a therapeutic community, a spiritual community, an activist community, a revolutionary cell, an avocational community, or any of the other groupings of persons seeking a good attainable through interaction with others.

A Learning Community generates a miniculture that values efficacious learning that may or may not be socially realized. All healthy communities render individuals who are secure; willing to take risks for personal and common goods; trusting of others; supportive of others;, and motivated by appropriate renditions of the motivating values of love of learning, love for each other, and, implicitly though necessarily, love of self.

Indeed, students note that they feel relaxed and at ease in the LCP situation, and yet the seemingly paradoxical realization dawns that they also experience themselves as critically challenged and critically responding in ways that they have not typically associated with classroom dynamics. From the perspective of LCP, however, the coemergence of a sense of relaxation and easefulness, combined with the experience of being critically self-challenged and, at the same time, invited to respond critically to others as well as to oneself, are key dynamics that are fully intended. The thesis is that critical learning becomes both more likely and more fulfilling in the context of personal security and interactional trust, which infuse student participation and professorial authority.

A probable reason that easefulness, trust, and security make critical learning and responsive selfing more likely is that critical learning and, at its deepest move, liberal education, is inherently threatening and, at times, downright scary; and this includes the professor as well as students. Tense sweat has often run down my spine during Learning Community sessions, especially when they took on a life of their own and moved in unanticipated directions. After all, liberal education and critical thinking indicate that the student strives to liberate self, since the professor cannot liberate anyone who does not wish to be liberated from conventional, familial, cultural, and psychological objectified certainties that have grounded the students' lives up to that point. To reject or reformulate or recover newer understandings for grounding one's life means, also, to reject or reformulate or recover the sources of those taken-for-granted truths and understandings, which include one's family standing, religious faith, nationalist idols, and whatever other authorities supplied the beliefs that anchored the students' senses of self up to that point. The seeming paradox of relaxation and critical learning is pedagogically not a paradox but a synergy.

The relaxation-critical learning link provides a pedagogical reason for the systematic presence and use of humor. Studies continue to show the physical and psychological advantages of humor and laughter, from lowering blood pressure to raising life expectancy. What LCP dynamics suggest is that humor and laughter also enhance critical learning, by soothing the threats and scariness of liberated education through sharing. Students leave able to laugh at the paradoxes of life and misrepresentations in what is taken for granted as the ways the world is working or the government is governing when unmasked—and thus seen as ideologically reenforcing accounts for the way those who make the rules, fashion the language, and advertise us to ourselves through products and media want the world to be for their own power and profit.

Laughter takes the fright out of the darkened closet by relativizing even darkness, through the light of a comedic moment or irruptions of disorder that paradoxically reaffirm the primacy of our quest for yet further order, fleeting though it must be in a world that continually changes, even as we come to know it—up till now. So LCP starts with a present participle—"learning"—that references not acquired knowledge, such as a concept or essence or facts or data, but the activity of acquiring knowledge, that is, an unending dynamic of coming to terms with how we look upon and think about what we take to be the world and ourselves within that presumably-known-as-seen world.

One pedagogical means that emerges from such easeful love of both learning and one another is that participants experience exchanges in which ego is separated from issue, even as self remains engaged with the issue and with others. Such paradoxically tensed and empowering "disengaged engagement" is central to LC dynamics. Participants acquire the presence and patterns of responding to criticisms of one's own statements, interpretations, or reasoning as affectively neutral processes that are not aimed at diminishing anyone present—a difficult interactional ideal.

Each participant's ideas or comments are reinterpreted as "objects" separate from self, even the self who proposed the object for the Learning Community to consider. The Learning Community learns to visualize and address these symbolic objects, as they symbolically lie in the center of the encircling class. As one student commented, it is easier to address issues, disagree with others' comments, and criticize statements if they are seen as freestanding objects, and not identified with the student or, especially, the professor who made the comments that enter into or even constitute the object in the middle of the discussion circle.

Creating an object out of students' and professors' comments allows space and objectivity for others to respond with what they are actually thinking, rather than maneuver to save one's standing, other students' egos, the professors' authority, or one's own risks for agreeing with or criticizing it. An object standing, as it were, in the middle of the class circle, mirrors the possibility of psychologically separating ego from issue and freeing students from interpersonal obstacles to freeflowing commentary.

The affectively freestanding object makes it easier for participants in the LC to respond with more spontaneous and relatively uncensored critical comments. To enact this critical engagement, while keeping issues at an aesthetic distance that allows uncensored scrutiny and risky responses, participants need to free themselves from the norms of "niceness," "mere opinion." or "pedestrian value relativity," which either dissuade or diminish their critical engagement.

Middle-class-and-up students manifest what one ethnographer (of their likely suburban origins) labeled "moral minimalism." Suburbanites do not engage each other in weighty moral issues, challenge each other's lifestyle directly, or introduce pivotal issues into the superficial sociality that seems to characterize much of suburban and, thus, modern middle-class-and-above lifestyles. Such moral minimalism emerges in classroom discussions as well. It comes in a variety of commandments: Thou shalt not make anyone uncomfortable; Thou shalt state mere opinions and define others' statements as merely their opinions; Thou shalt not directly challenge anyone's statements or constructed objects, neither those of other students nor, above all else, those of professors; Thou shalt not commit the sin of showing personal interest in the issue; Thou shalt always speak in that disembodied, aloof "student voice" that symbolizes disengagement from the interaction; Thou shalt commit apathy through body language and posture that announces indifference.

Like becoming a religious saint or philosophical stoic, easefully separating Ego from Issue is a challenge of a lifetime that allows for much growth, to the extent that self is committed, others are supportive, and the excitement of shared learning is experienced at least as a possibility and, occasionally, with a burst of Ah Ha! All participants, especially the professor, must strive to separate Ego from Issue. As trust in the group grows, if it does, statements are gradually experienced as just that, as objects for critical examination and not as criticisms of self or other, or of anyone's personal worth or standing in the Learning Community. Ego is no longer the Issue. Of course, complete uncoupling of Ego and Issue is never totally attained, since statements by self always contain something of self's standing that can be appreciated or unappreciated. The struggle to separate Ego and Issue is a lifetime task. (I still fail after a lifetime spent trying to treat statements as Issues and not Ego, though ancient wisdom teaches that our voice exposes our soul, and it is not what goes into the mouth that sullies a person but what comes out of it.)

So, for example, learning communities organized around perennial human concerns—such as nature, society, self, and understandings of God—or, more specifically, around critical contemporary issues—such as personal and species identity and human-environment mutual sustainability—provide cognitive and emotional space and engagement, in which all earthbound humans share, whether they recognize their dependence on the issues or not. In other words, Learning Community arises around issues that are universal and inclusive: All participants share in the issues, and the issues are generalizable to all who live within the dependencies of the globe, whether they know and ontologize these dependencies or not. A defining goal, then, of a Learning Community is to bring all participants to see and to posit the dependencies and the issues of human impact on these dependencies that all share. An "earthling" identity hopefully emerges that incorporates even one's religious or citizen identity and opens all identities to critical and discussable dimensions.

Shared understandings of common issues and common dependencies hopefully generate a shared sense of wonder that elicits a need to know, which empowers the right and desire to learn together with others who share the same issues. In the face of such shared issues, however, each participant retains, fosters, and comes to realize his or her own set of supportive values and styles of learning. Each learner is empowered in a personal way in support of common themes.

Meditation V: Learning Community Emerges From Shared Understandings

Shared understandings among participants in a Learning Community arise within a context of mini Towers of Babel. Assume in class that virtually everyone speaks the same language yet virtually no one intends to say exactly what he or she is thinking; virtually no one is capable of saying exactly what he or she is thinking, even if the speaker wishes to be "perfectly clear;" and regardless of the intentional efficacy and linguistic mastery of the speaker, virtually no one listening will understand totally what is said and, *a fortiori*, no one will know what it is the speaker is really thinking.

A message sent is not identical to the message received. Additionally, the act of sending one's thinking in a message leads to a rethinking of the message: Thinking and speaking are interfused processes. A typical student reaction to one's speaking is a qualification such as "I'm still working this out," or even "I'm not sure what I mean." In other words, Learning Community arises from the ashes of unformed thoughts; ill-stated thinking; inadequate interpretation by others; and a guiding as well as a misleading sense of opposition or agreement. Many of these limitations to communication are general but limited. In a Learning Community, however, they are of the essence, and far more inclusive as shared experiences.

Underlying shared understandings, then, is a major dynamic of translation through linguistic as well as metalinguistic—or body language—forms of communication, each with its own clarities and obfuscations. Translation here is taken in a broad sense: It is difficult, open-ended, and never finished or univocal. In any single translation, the adage "Much is lost in translation" is true. Furthermore, much is often added; and if the losses and additions amplify each other, then translation negates shared understanding. So shared understanding may be a shared subjective illusion, manipulated misleading, or well-meant *faux pas* with unknown consequences—but not efficacious knowledge as a goal of the Learning Community. Think of a Learning Community arising among those with the greatest differences that separate them: Fundamentalists and Progressives; Israeli Orthodox and Palestinian Militants; or even Democrats and Republicans.

Yet in a classroom, a Learning Community may arise among individuals with rather homogeneous and restricted cultural backgrounds, sets of values, and languages, again taken widely. Shared learning emerges along with engagement and competence in a shared language. Translation of one's subjective apprehension of the world, and interpretations of the same into a discourse from which others can both learn that subjectively-grounded perspective and align it with their own, requires that participants speak the same language in a situated, contextual, and interpretive sense. Sure, all speak English (or another common language), but assuming that a common language leads to shared discourse is a probability upon which many a group, even a married couple, has foundered.

A major task of the teacher/learner in LCP, then, is to foster mutual reinterpretations of what speakers are intending and what others take as what was intended. This is a walk across eggshells. It involves trust and security on everyone's part. The speaker must be open to a reworking of what he or she thought self was saying. In the competitive, superficial, competency-default norm of a judgmental institutional contest to achieve deliberately rationed payoffs—aka grades—students initially resist having their thoughts worked by others; and, more deeply, many students resist reworking their own way of thinking. To do so is tantamount to admitting

"I was wrong, stupid, ignorant, incompetent, inadequate"—fill in your favorite word of self-recrimination upon receiving a public "correction" and threat of an inferior grade. Imagine, then, the challenge of accepting the norm that no one knows everything; that every speaker is to some degree launching into an unknown—the end of the sentence is implicated in its beginning; but classical writers had already developed the anacoluthon to grasp the disconnected, emergent, creative, and, to a degree, self-correcting nature of discourse-in-action. Contemporary discourse analysis shows self-correction as intrinsic to conversation as a process as well as to utterances as an act. Eventually learners, in addition to acquiring content, learn even as they are speaking and dialoguing; and, of course, so must the person identified as "teacher."

Translation, then, is a multilayered and widely-faceted task of restating each putatively subjective perspective into the intersubjective discourse shared by all; and by a sort of alchemy, what was subjective becomes intersubjective and, thus, socially speaking, objective. The task of assessing the adequacy, empirically, descriptively, and scientifically, of the now-objectified understandings remains the crux of socially realized knowledge, as humans work toward sustainable futures in relation to their physical and cultural environments.

Translation appears to work to a degree among students even within the boundaries of a semester-long or year-long seminar that meets but twice weekly. This is not to say that everyone agrees with everyone else on even a single issue. It does suggest, however, that learners acquire additional information, alternative perspective for making sense of always-inadequate information, and a sense of self-correction, other-correction, and social-efficaciousness as a desideratum of knowledge in a realist sense. Even these modest shared learnings appear unlikely at global levels or at interstices of hateful boundaries or fields of conflict. Yet pedagogy is a practice that engages in desirable shared futures, not reactionary exclusivist pasts. In a word, pedagogy is a practice within idealism, illustrated by the literature of utopias, but with a subscript of pragmatic possibility.

Translation, in the dual language and self-awareness senses mentioned here, implies that all "fundamentalisms" are then rendered either contingent or less than exhaustively serious or exclusivist. Learners recast their forever or recent unquestioned certitudes in terms of the method and interactional realization of perspectivizing their subjective apprehension of the world and resultant interpretation of what that apprehension means. Perspectivizing does not mean abandonment. It means that self's view is now known simultaneously with knowledge that others—as fully human as oneself—have both different apprehensions and interpretations, perhaps even more adequate apprehensions and more plausible yet contradictory interpretations. These realizations relativize one's worldview, not necessarily in the sense that it is erroneous, but simply that it is not synonymous with a fully human grasp of the world and its meanings. Learners may, after going through the matrix of self-awareness and interactional emergence, retain their previous views of the world's meanings (they cannot go back to asserting that their apprehension of the world exhausts the empirical givenness of that world); and they also certainly retain their previous beliefs in transcendental realities not subject to apprehension and empirical sharing. They go back to those beliefs and values, however, with an awareness of self- possession in passive and active senses of what they take to be knowledge of the world.

Such self-other possession of what is taken as the world and its meanings defangs all fundamentalisms of their pseudo legitimacy to justify violence against anyone solely on the basis of one's own perspective. Fundamentalisms include any unquestioned form of the world that one takes as a total closed and certain explanation that includes even those who do not accept that unquestioned form. It is a form of cognitive-affective reductionism that substitutes my experience for that of the other; mine is valid, the other's is mistaken and has no right to exist. So, for example, religious and quasireligious fundamentalisms stand out as the most common historical instances of total, exclusivist, and transcendental worldviews.

All totalist ideologies, as grand master and exclusivist narratives of the world and its inhabitants, fall into the fundamentalism that does violence to other and one's own search for a virtuous life. Fundamentalisms include all *aprioris* that are accepted as totally explaining the world; Platonic fallacies that mistake my forms for knowing the world with the world in itself; Scholastic essences that are given existence as "*entia realia*" rather than as "*entia mentalia*"; Cartesian clear and distinct ideas that work like algebraic entities within a conceptual space mistakenly taken as the space that curves around us; Newtonian constructs made into scientific universals that calculate only as far as their reduced space/time boundaries extend. Contemporary forms that are difficult to see, because we see with them as lenses, include unbridled capitalism-as-culture; optimistic technologism; shortterm American primacy; and free-market dynamics to adjudicate distribution of goods and services clandestinely woven with power interests, which work outside of public accountability to pirate profits in extra-market and after-hour manipulations.

Today's world follows the Einsteinian, ecological, nuclear, microbiochemical, and nanocyber revolutions that render prior forms of the world as historical relics, and the search for efficacious knowledge endlessly complex and precarious. Fuzzy, fractured thinking laced with affective ribs and seams, when applied ineluctably, brings about unintended and often unforeseen effects, which then present the calculus for human species knowledge and joint actions. Our knowledge is always what a German word for "concept" metaphorically depicts: a grasping, *"ein Begriff,"* which holds the world but briefly and mistaken in the shape of the hand/mind/heart that does the grasping.

Translation, then, involves a search for shared understandings across multiple levels of communication. Language is the key symbolic medium, dynamic, dimension, and content for LCP, though not the only one. Language arises within a context punctuated with bodily movements, postures, and lapses. The very activation of language, furthermore, paradoxically gives rise to the mysterious communication generated by group silence—a silence that sometimes cries out for interpretation even as it affirms a mood, underlines a quandary, or highlights a shared doomsday, much as a burst of laughter sometimes communicates a dialectical mix of these meanings.

To address and connect with the levels of self-identities and experiences of student learners, LCP ranges widely across sociolinguistic types of narrative, actual discourse, and talk styles. Talk and ways of speaking link students' identities with language categories and what are sometimes called "sociomental" communities, that is, groups of speakers with shared identities and shared ways of seeing, interpreting, valuing, and feeling about what they take to be the world in which they live.

At least four modes of socially situated language are functional for LCP. First, properly formal and pedantic academic discourse connects students with vocabularies and modes of reasoning and analysis that are beyond the comfort zone, if not grasp, of many students up till now. Second, biographical prose incorporates lived experiences of the teacher who is, in the age-graded context of the classroom, almost always older and often much older than the students. Third, values and humanistic issues come clothed in discourses of desirable futures and universal yearnings of human needs and wishes. Wishful thinking and thinkful wishing are carried in languages of sought-for relief and ennobling possibility. Finally, LCP at times approaches the folk language of Anglo-Saxonisms, sometimes with four letters, of the street and backstage areas, in comparison with the institutional formalisms of educational "class" present through the built-classroom setting.

These walkways, roadways, mediaways, pubways, and backstage venues are places in which the emotional highs and lows and extremes of student lives are sometimes experienced. Although they are not of the classroom, they are relevant to the classroom, if the classroom is to be relevant to the humane range of learning that is a goal of LCP. One purpose of folk, even foul, Anglo-Saxon is to semantically, cognitively, and evocatively bridge the often normative disconnect between classroom learning and learning to deal in one or another of students' everyday worlds. LCP avowedly, if indirectly, by talk and example and value, and at times directly, by challenges about what to eat, drink, smoke, and play, forges a connection between these domains of students' lives.

To overcome the disconnect between academic classroom discourse, a professor in LCP may at times dip into "foul" language, though students are not allowed, through gentle reminders that the professor's foul or Anglo-Saxon language is part of pedagogy: The professor already possesses academic and disciplinary language proficiencies to name, apprehend, distinguish, analyze, and more or less adequately express what he or she intends, though always with the anacoluthon freedom to continually rephrase and restate thoughts that are continually emerging. Ranging over the sociostyles of language, students hopefully acquire the openness and analogic capability to see how issues expressed in academic and disciplinary and proper classroom discourse are actually similar, relevant, and applicable to their so-called real lives in their families, dorms, drinking excursions, and other youthful experimentations that are part of personal and social development as they experience life. In brief, translation enables learners not only to acquire new knowledge and perspectives from others and to restate their subjective understandings in a more expansive and objective intersubjective frame, but also to translate experiences in one dimension of their lives into other dimensions, and also, perhaps, to achieve a more valued sense of integration and focus in their understandings of themselves and the trajectories of their lives into futures ever just beyond their reach—a secular experience of "Else what is heaven for!"

The translation function, taken in a wide sense, works across the boundaries of the formatting of the time spent when the LC gathers together. Readings assigned to be done before class for the most part are in disciplinary discourse and fairly technical language that brings its own power to probe vertically into issues, with its own limitations of assumptions and reductionisms that define technical analyses. Readings ideally provide a shared disciplinary matrix and content for classroom discussion. The discussion presumably is based on the assumption that everyone is to some degree familiar with the readings' issues and contents.

Meditation VI: Formatting a Learning Community Pedagogy

There is a simple descriptive pattern to this kind of LCP. Class begins with time given to addressing issues of "housekeeping," a phase of class time borrowed from my spouse's—aka my Earthmate's—successful teaching techniques. The opening statement, initially said by the professor and then by student "catalysts" energizing the discussion always is, "Does anyone have any housekeeping items?" Housekeeping refers to any issue, experience, or current happening that concerns us as LCP participants. Mostly, references are to current events available through media, typically newspapers or TV, or to personal experiences or observations, such as interpersonal exchanges, events on campus, or communication with parents. Housekeeping reenforces growing group awareness forming a sense of collective identity, with events now relevant to self because self is a member of the LC. Furthermore, it helps bridge the disconnect between classroom and life writ as wide as students typically live it. Housekeeping is translation at work, as students learn to apply classroom tools to reconceptualize and reaestheticize what occurs within their and others' experiences here and now. This dynamic is referenced by the phrase, "The world is our classroom."

Housekeeping also opens time/space for the professor to introduce current events relevant to issues from prior discussions, or to anticipate likely upcoming issues. Copies of newspaper clippings may be handed out for evaluative, critical, and analytic responses. Even limited to the lofty international and national scope of pieces from the *New York Times* and local community issues and happenings from a local paper, instances relevant to themes of nature, society, self, God, environment, and identity occur with refreshing frequency, if not always positive implications. Housekeeping moments may run for the entire class, as one student remarked with a mild sense of frustration and irony. Indeed, one such event, the declaration by the then- Governor of California that the drought had ended there thanks to God and the people of California, developed into a lengthy collective reflection about the meaning of drought ending, and appeals to Divinity in social and environmental causality.

So LCP format starts with housekeeping. There was an earlier version of inchoate LCP that began with the query, "Any questions?" This was a borrowing from one of the most evocative and efficacious courses taken by this ex-Jesuit professor during his philosophical studies while still in the Order. At this university, however, over many years, the only questions asked about procedural issues involved papers, exams, and grading policy. Students in this inchoate LC rarely if ever asked a substantive question. Some other lead-in was needed to bridge the disconnect between students' sense of academic classroom learning and their personal and social experiences. Housekeeping by the professor and eventually by students helps make that connection, which may empower students to reformulate and reaestheticize their daily lives.

Formatting LCP includes occasional visual or audial presentations, such as videos or museum visits, which introduce another layer of symbolic communication that is more fuzzy, inclusive, or evocative—characteristics that complement the clear, exclusive, analytic strengths of disciplinary discourse. After housekeeping, which occasionally takes up major segments of our time together, LCP proceeds with typically two student catalysts assigned to energize a discussion of the readings.

Different groups generate different cultural responses to "catalyzing." Some break into small groups, a few think up an exercise to illustrate an issue in the readings, most play it straight with questions hopefully eliciting responses. Often the questions are nondiscussable, vaguely unfocused, or framed as opinion gleaning. An indirect kind of learning may emerge from these experiences, as students discern what kinds of questions are ripe for discussion and which are too green or already past their prime. Punctuating class discussion are periodic professorial presentations of "board work," which provide a visual summary of issues, concepts, and mostly analytic schema that offer conceptual frameworks for analyzing a standard issue within the content area of the course.

Students come to appreciate a classical rhetorical frame that enables communication to continue in the face of obvious, ever-present inadequacies of expression, namely, the mutatis *mutandis* principle for interpreting the relevance and robustness of anyone's statement: The hearkener, or active loving listener, changes whatever needs to be adjusted to make the statement reasonable, robust, and relevant. Out of translatable self-other discourse arises the possibility of a fuller humanity gained through shared experiences.

Finally, freedom is a founding principle informing everyone's participation in the Learning Community. Given the authority arrangements of a college class, which make students' fates subject to the power of the professor—a power ultimately anchored in the act of bestowing a permanently recorded and quasipublic grade—freedom is particularly relevant to students' participation in the Learning Community. And it takes time, often too much time for a single semester, for the students to trust that the professor really means freedom (within the limits of larger cultural constraints, since freedom is not license) for students as well as for the professor. For example, occasionally the professor asks for a circular response to an issue, that is, students around the circle take turns commenting or reflecting on an issue. In this exercise, as in all forms of interactional participation, students are free to respond or not, and always without prejudice, that is, they retain the unpenalized free option "to pass" and not respond.

Students' realization of participation freedom is premised on their trust in, for example, the professor's assurance that availing oneself of this freedom is not graded. Again, LCP structures space for students' free participation and risk-taking, as they gain trust that the dynamics of the group focus on their learning, and not primarily and exhaustively on their being evaluated and graded. Concomitant with students activating trust in the professor is the contextual trust in other students. This is a subtle and unlabeled foundation for LCP, and one that appears to emerge gradually, if at all. Students must learn to trust other students, as well as the professor and their own selves, for the pedagogy to be effective. This is a major source of my anxiety during the first few weeks of a semester, since it is never certain if efficacious trust will indeed emerge. Fortunately, I am able to count untrusting LCs on a few fingers of one hand.

Participatory freedom for all in the Learning Community is another dynamic that gives less interactional control to the professor. Less control, however, does not necessarily translate into a loss of control or a weaker class. Freedom generates a different dynamic within the class and opens the possibilities for different contexts of experiencing and learning; at the least, there is the probability of additional desirable outcomes, kinds of learning that elicit critical rearranging of students' received ways of seeing and thinking about the world and their places in it.

The loss of control does make class dynamics more risky, in the sense that the professor does not know what will happen next, which issues will emerge in the discussions, whether the professor's weighting of topics and approaches will dominate, or even whether the professor will be recognized as the expert in areas of new and unplanned issues and concerns that emerge from students' own agendas.

Indeed, I have congratulated students for a "break out" class when I judged that they moved beyond socially desirable or formal classroom etiquette and criteria to express what they really believed about an issue. My judgment, in such instances, typically was based on the intensity of students' involvement in the discussion—an involvement seen through body language, felt by the conviction of expression, heard and known in the words chosen to express their perceptions, and manifested in a chorus, if not cacophony, of plural voices engaging the object(s) under construction.

The loss of univocal, authoritarian control by a professor willing to run the risk opens space for more student spontaneity in class interaction. More spontaneity generates more surprises. More surprises transforms classes from a known and predictable domain of rote, routine, unifocused professorial performances into an unknown, unpredictable domain of Learning Community adventures. Class as *adventure* means that no one, including the professor, knows what will emerge and even what will "happen" in any given class! Entering an adventure, for this temperamentally risk-aversive professor, may explain why sweat runs down his spine, dews his armpits, and moistens his palms while chilling his fingers during many classes! Such is the conviction and also the price of this mode of LCP. Class-as-adventure is sometimes translated into student subcultural cant as confusing, eventually challenging, and occasionally "fun." It is not necessarily so for the institutional carrier of the final authority and responsibility, however. It is a risky adventure empirically driven by the quality and mix of student personas.

Meditation VII: What May a Learning Community Professor Profess?

An underlying principle for LCP is that humans face an historically new critical context. For the first time in history, humans are, through dominant institutional arrangements, significant actors affecting species survival globally, not only regionally or locally. Historically, analysts suggest that humans, like other animals, have affected their environmental niches locally. They and all animals have been "ecosystemic actors." Ecosystemic actors change their local and regional environments primarily, with no likely longterm effects on global environmental dynamics.

Today, however, there is solid reason to accept the description of human actions on the environment as those of "biospheric actors." That is, human activities are now recognized as significant, perhaps pivotal, causes of global environmental changes. As the empirical description of human activity as biospheric in its effect gains recognition, apparently to the point of scientific consensus, the issue moves to interpretations and evaluations of the changes with the imperative of responding to them. Okay, so human activity is changing global environmental patterns in thus far chronic and rather gradual patterns, such as climate change, global warming, rising ocean levels, and the bioaccumulation of synthetic chemicals in the water and food chains.

Some analysts, however, suggest a probability greater than zero that such gradual and chronic changes may trigger a threshold or tipping point and generate a rupture in current environmental dynamics. This suggestion seems to reflect the theoretical idea of punctuated equilibrium in evolutionary reconstructions. Furthermore, continual development of weapons of mass destruction that work at ever deeper levels of organic, chemical, and physical intervention present humans with a probability of an acute and abrupt change in the ability of local ecosystems to sustain higher life; and, depending on the scope of mass destruction, perhaps, again, a probability greater than zero of triggering a global outcome akin to descriptions of a "nuclear winter," following a sufficiently damaging exchange of nuclear weapons. Accompanying the warfare probabilities are those of nuclear accidents *à la* Three Mile Island or Chernobyl. Such accidents may even become "normal accidents" that result from contradictions and inefficiencies in complex bureaucratic institutions, which lead to higher likelihoods of unintended outcomes, such as malfunctioning airbags in cars and exploding oil wells in the Caribbean. A defining issue, then, is whether these changes are better or worse for human sustainability.

The debate is being joined over chronic and, thus far, gradual environmental changes. No one, at least as far as I know at the time of this writing, has argued that widespread use of weapons of mass destruction or normal accidents are human goods. For example, contrary to the understanding of a weapon that threatens the lives of those who are an undesirable threat to us, weapons of mass destruction aim not at personnel solely but at the systems that support their lives. So, for example, the classical understanding of war as the extension of state policy toward others by militaristic means in order to achieve a rational goal, such as conquest and defense, is rendered at times contradictory: Who "wins" a nuclear contaminated territory? There are a number of parties, however, who seem to believe that they can use weapons of mass destruction for some moral self-interest or even common good; and these parties include not only terrorists and so-called "evil regimes," but even self-defined democratic and moral nation-states, including our own.

No need here to try to unpack the myriad issues that weapons of mass destruction, normal accidents, and ecological threats raise for collective and cooperative human responses. Suffice it to say that the issues have a major impact on the meanings of our students' lives, and that many of them appear sufficiently, even deeply, aware of possible implications for them across the range of their interpretations, from religious faith and moral decisions to the levels of stress and futurity they sense in their lives. The issues and their problematic progeny elicit the full range of reflection and policy formation, in the face of an historically new and globally ubiquitous set of issues that face us in our species being, which perhaps includes survival and sustainability.

A second issue calling for our professing is that of contemporary personal and group identity formation, motivations, and enactments. Identity lies at the crossing point of the "cross" that every human carries in his or her head and heart. The contemporary context, with global environmental interventions and weapons of mass destruction availabilities, make the issue of identity, and its own progeny problems, more critical than ever before. The Hatfields and McCoys feuding over back pathways, or even boundary squabbling nation-states, until now could work out their identity conflicts without putting many, perhaps most, and imaginably everyone else, at added risk of danger or death.

Today, identity issues, especially those with transcendental referents and legitimations, need to be reweighted, reprioritized, and rendered into the service of, and not antagonistic to, more inclusivist species identities. From its historical function of defining self—and most typically, self as a member of a group and subject to group think—students today need to discover ways to sustain their personal and group identities, while fitting them in relevant ways into larger species identities, e.g., environmental identities or, as a university president has been heard to say, global identities that define each of us in terms that include all of us, to the exclusion of no one. Globally activating this type of inclusivist identity in efficacious collective actions would be something new on the face of this earth. Learning such activation is not gossamer-utopian daydreaming but the very stuff of ennobling our collective efforts to respond to shared issues and solve—always for the time being—common problems, only to readdress them in the next phase of history.

LCP accepts these issues; each learner may add his and her own for the lifetimes of our students. Thus, learning must, in relevant ways, concern students with their biographical and societal version of the perennial human task of learning to live in the only space available, Earth, and in the only time given to them and all of us, Now.

The kind of knowledge informing LCP contrasts with the specialized and, to that extent, reductionist, though powerful, knowledge generated within disciplinary and *apriori* frameworks. Such specialized, framed, and structured disciplines of knowledge are indispensible to human efforts to intervene in social relations, group dynamics, societal interrelationships, and, issues involving natural environments. LCP engages in more general and experiential sharing of what each and all may take to be knowledge here and now, that is, a mutually satisfactory view of the world in this situation, so that collective action will be undertaken to respond to the embedded issue that engages the community here and now. In other words, LCP engages in both disciplinary scientific knowledge forged within empirical engagement with a salient and implicated aspect of the world, and—more existentially and with more difficulty—in efficacious knowledge that informs a collective response to a mutually shared issue/problem that transforms difference and conflict into mutuality and cooperation, to the extent of the universality implicated in the shared issue/problem.

Implicated in such efficacious knowledge relevant to material and environmental issues is the concomitant recognition of mutual and shared identities generated by each group's and person's relation to the issue/problem. Efficacious knowledge, in a word, generates and derives from emerging awareness of shared identities. For example, since all humans are dependent on air, water, food, energy, animals, and arable soil, it is eventually in everyone's identity interests to sustain those life-supporting resources. Note again, the need for empirically-embedded identity sources and destinies: Beware of the world-denying power of transcendentally-anchored identities, whether in religious or ideological frameworks. LCP sees both human-environment and human-human dialectics as interwoven issues in the emerging world of global communication, travel, food, and materials transport, as well as air-soil-water-food systemic production cum threats.

Highlighting themes such as chronic and acute environmental interventions and the sameness-difference, togetherness-violence of personal and group identities may seem too dark, depressing, or pessimistic. Quite the contrary: LCP is also informed by the need and quest for sources of hope. Social hope, as some philosophers put it, is a pragmatic stance that addresses the need for knowledge to inform right action. Postmodern awareness challenges individualist, group, ideological, and religious certitudes and universalist foundations to knowing and acting. The only method, or metapathway, as the Greek metaphors for informing the root of method suggests, is mutual intelligence that generates shared understandings to underwrite collectively sustainable efficacious actions.

Meditation VIII: This-Worldly Hope Informs Learning Community Pedagogy

How is it that focusing on what some see as depressing themes of environment and identity, and perennial human concerns with interpretations of nature, society, self, and God, generates "this-worldly" sources of hope? LCP is not catechism or revelation or any transcendent answer to human issues—thus the qualifier "this-worldly."

Social hope is a version of what humans traditionally referred to as "knowledge of the world." No one's "knowledge" appears as knowledge to those who do not accept the presenter's framework and assumptions. As has been said, what is knowledge on one side of the Pyrenees, the Jordan River, the Red Sea, or the Atlantic is error on the other. The globalization of people's intermingling and communication renders older versions of individual, group, or even disciplinary knowledge inefficacious, unless translated into weapons of mass destruction and used to impose one's knowledge on another. Religious faith as knowledge for living served in a pre-modern world; ideological market logic and democratic involvement served piecemeal to generate the modern world; neither is adequate to a postmodern world that generates not local identities or local ecosystem issues but global inclusion and biospheric threats as the issues.

Social hope, then, is a functional equivalent for previous forms and dynamics of what was taken as knowledge. Social hope aims at efficacious knowledge based, as best we can, on verisimilitude forms of empirical and scientific knowledge in the received sense of those terms. Social hope commits participants to trust in each other, to focus on relevant issues salient for all, and to rely on shared intellect—the method of intelligence in contrast with interest-grounded reason, interest-serving ideologies, or posited transcendent payoffs dependent on nonempirical acts of faith in a symbolic constructed world.

Social hope enables humans to act collectively as if they are informed by shared knowledge. The "knowledge" emerges as the best that the group can agree upon; it is not necessarily the best representation or picture of the world, but the best that enables members of the group to engage in cooperative action toward a mutually necessary goal. So, for example, issues of environmental sustainability based on life-support systems of air, water, soil, food, and energy, along with the many biochemical "cycles" that sustain life, are shared necessary resources for continued human survival. So too, issues of identity sustainability based on social-psychological processes of producing and internalizing meanings that give value and sense to personal existence is always dependent on generative and supportive group identities. Both must be sustained and simultaneously enlarged to include those of others who are not like us physically or symbolically. In the reduction of environmental and symbolic spaces of the postmodern global world, traditional meanings that sustained personal and group identities included a strong aversive and differentiating dynamic that affirmed "I am not You!" and more to the point, "We are not They!"

In today's world, such aversive differentiating identifiers based on the "other" as "totally other" and framed in its negativity toward self are no longer functional and are increasingly dangerous. The historically most powerful symbol system is the aversive power of religion, especially religion merged with the primordial biological markers of gender, race, and ethnicity. We see such a combination dividing our contemporary world into the fundamentalisms of Christian, Jew, Muslim and various combinations that legitimate actions affirming self by eliminating the other.

The viability of eliminative and exclusivist religions as the sole or main functional identity for self and group no longer serves the environmental and identity issues of today's world. Each religious tradition needs to look within itself for species-inclusivist criteria and logics that enable those who derive their identities from that tradition to engage all humans in meaningful participation in communities that strive to solve issues of collective survival and personal fulfillment.

Species-inclusivist identity formation needs to replace tribal-exclusivist structures within even the so-called universalist religious traditions. The latter too often keep a strong, aversive identity dynamic within its self understanding, whether based on the scandal of particularity, as John Courtney Murray stated about Christianity, or some transcendental claim to unique possession of certitude and truth—even revealed directly from the Divinity to ancestors within a religious tradition. The task is to render religions based on aversive, identity dynamics more open to environmental and identity participation in shared and mutual relations, with believers within other traditions. The creedal content of faith claims, in other words, must be subordinated to the inclusivist love and mercy potential, to reference Pope Francis, and to the inclusivist social hope of pragmatic movements within the traditions. To paraphrase St. Paul, there are faith, hope, and love, and the greatest two of these are universal love and inclusivist hope!

A goal for LCP within my faith-based university, for example, a Catholic-Christian university, then, is to pursue faith seeking understanding, *"fides quaerens intellectum,"* which is made relevant to the postmodern global world and its profound challenges, including those of environment and identity. *Fides* arises with the particularism of the historical tradition. Now, more than ever before, this particularistic *fides* must seek not simply "ratio" or reason within another system but *"intellectum"* that looks for both means-end rationality and, more efficaciously, collective action toward new systems of living on the earth and with one another. *Intellectus* is the inclusivist and truly universalist basis for social hope. *Fides* and ratio are derivative values that must be subordinated to species survival and empirical fulfillment. These themes are meditative derivations, from a Christian incarnational theological perspective, that start with the natural world as God's first and foundational revelation and shared intellect as God's natural means for discovering the Divinity and moral code that precedes historical claims of particularistic traditions. The intellect of LCP starts with the world as it is mutually present to those who act upon it and with each other. All *aprioris*, as inheritances from the past, must be rethought and reworked in learning communities concerned with mutually imagined futures, in which all have a stake and from which all can derive social hope for themselves and their children.

LCP remains within the empirical, scientific, and even incarnational realm of the experientially available world. It is further grounded on the premise that this-worldly sources of hope that appeal to all is a necessary component within democratic learning. Such hope would be a nondistributive species emergent: Showing hope enhances hope. Unlike the scarcity endemic to material possessions, but rather like knowledge, hope shared by all would be enhanced, not diminished, the more it is shared. As a good that intrinsically invites others to recognize and experience it, hope must arise as an outcome of an authentic shared species characteristic. You guessed it—for LCP that universal characteristic is intellect in action, the ability to define shared issues and analyze the common problems that arise from those issues.

Empirically relevant hope informing LCP is distinct from both religiously based hope in a transcendent, other-worldly resolution to this world's issues and ideologically based presumptions, which believe all issues and resultant problems would be resolved if only all persons and societies subordinated themselves to one reductionist *apriori* theory or model, such as bureaucratic centralism or market decentralism. Recall that within traditional Christian teaching, hope is one of the three theological virtues appropriate for a creature. Recall, too, that the contrary sins against hope are not only the hot sin of despair, which our optimistic culture repudiates so loudly, but also the cold sin of presumption, which our optimistic culture reifies as an unquestioned certitude. Believing that one has the certain answer to life's future is neither intellectually defensible nor empirically demonstrable; and in a traditional Christian worldview, it is actually a sinful attitude toward life and providence. One does not hear much of the disorientation or sin that is presumption, an attitude that destroys the virtue of hope because it transforms it into either a certitude or an unreasonable gullibility that informs false hope released from Pandora's Box as a bane on human life.

Meditation IX: Learning about Teaching in a Learning Community

A Learning Community refers to a pedagogy based on interaction and an emergent group culture. The interaction is based on a universal good—the exercise of critical intelligence as at once a primary personal good as well as an evolutionary species good for survival and shared living.

The root metaphor of a community is living within common walls or fortifications. Like the walled cities of human-built environments, community creates empirically available safe space and time to pursue shared goals that both realize personal needs and make shared aspirations likely outcomes. Communities share, then, a love—in a totally secular and apt sense as desire for goods that enable all to live together in common space and time—the inherent tension of our beastly angelic natures as simultaneously individual and social selves. Love for shared goals brings members of a Learning Community into common space and time for learning how to live meaningful lives together.

Sources of LC formation are new, assigned texts, such as reading, viewing, and listening to scheduled inputs. Functioning as metaphorical "texts" are each participant's biographical experiences, many of which are already shared in parallel-play fashion by other members of the student's age cohort; the emergent shared experiences of the Learning Community during its time together, an advantage that grows in yearlong seminars; and the elder experiences of the professor who is from a prior-age cohort and set of historical events and experiences. This at least bimodal cohort experience lends some historicity to the emergent group culture. In more heterogeneous educational groups, the historical range of formative experiences would enrich the emergent group culture and nascent identity, ephemeral though it may be. At its root, the Learning Community realizes a professorial or institutional set of materials combined with individual student and professor responses, and an emerging group understanding of perennial "objects," that is, issues, values, understandings and commitments. The motoric is interaction fueled by a "student driven agenda."

"Community" is a social category and functional metaphor for understanding the dynamics underlying this pedagogy. Given the shared time/space of our coming together, below are selected social features relevant to a pedagogically situated "community" that may or may not emerge within the rather formal structure, learned expectations, students' and professors' life situations, and above all, the particular mix of personal biographies and historical pressures and definitions whirling within any LC and influencing each of us.

1. An informing principle refers to a defining relationship within an LC: We come together with a commitment of love of learning and of each other in ways relevant to learning.

2. One goal for realizing this principle is to attempt eloquence that expresses critical intelligence in pursuit of universal human values. This goal is discernible through intellectual lenses, typically organized around disciplinary perspectives such as literature, natural and social sciences, ecology, etc. Each perspective allows us to apply intelligence in disciplined ways that highlight selected aspects of the human condition and its circumstances. Perspectivity allows us to see and to know that about which—and the way through which—the disciplines focus our minds' eyes and informs our intellects and judgments. We formulate the products of disciplined perspectival knowing into appropriate genres, formats, and texts. As knowers, we assume that the more disciplines and genres at the disposal of the community, the better the community

can interpret its circumstances and each other, and formulate mutually agreeable descriptions of present situations and scenarios of desirable futures. Since human knowing is perspectival, in contrast to presumed divine knowledge, which would be omni-perspectival, we remain with feet on the ground, so our asymptotic approach to divine knowing is to share in the life of intellectual searching for personal as well as collective hope, a communal endeavor.

3. A guiding operational principle is continually to strive cognitively and affectively to separate ego from issue; ego from issue-become-object, in the center of the LC circle; and ego from ego's own expression. The whole person-in-community engages in a continuous process of "analysis, decision, and expression," the moments of intellect, value, and eloquence. And we do this together, in common, with and toward a common life. An utterance always carries a birthmark: It is mine, the speaker's. So, too, the speaker remains within the utterance, which is vivified by its personal genesis and group reception.

Community-based intellectual dynamic requires that the speaker uncouple self from statement, ego from issue. Such uncoupling allows self and others to treat the issue-object in the center of the circle as just that, and not a symbol of the worth, security, or personal standing of the speaker. In the etiquette that announces emerging norms of the LC, no statement is embarrassing or personally wrong. There are no *ad hominem* implications, and thus no *ad hominem* attacks, statements, or perceived attacks on statements.

Objects in center circle are there for analysis, decision, and expression, as the LC reconstructs them. They are there for our understanding, critique, and more generalized reformulation. Any statement about the objects may be accepted or rejected, as we work out reasons for our responses. Persons who express the objects, however, remain outside our intellectual reconstruction aimed only at the objects. Persons are neither in center circle nor objects of the community's intellectual work. Selves remain inviolable, as they make up the circle that creates the time/space for objective analysis, in every sense in which members of the community can make objects and be objective.

4. The "learning" in LC Pedagogy is to learn what it taken as *efficacious knowledge* and how to seek it, how to share it, and how to frame it. Learning is a lifelong process of generating what each participant believes is knowledge, and to relate it to how he or she believes and we ought to live.

LC Pedagogy defines knowledge as that which is objective, in contrast to what I experience as my subjective grasp of the world as I believe it is, and of my action as I believe it ought to be, to the extent that I believe I am in control of what I think is and ought to be.

Objectivity, however, is always social. It is a frame we use to translate what we believe into taken-for-granted knowledge of how the world works. In today's culture of individualism, objectivity is thought to be a possession of the individual mind. LC Pedagogy notes that we may find and locate objective knowledge in individual minds, but it is not our individuality that bestows the characteristic of knowing the object—being objective—on our knowledge. Rather, LC Pedagogy assumes that what each of us takes as an objective view of the world, to the extent that it is verifiably objective, is—in genesis and verification—intersubjective. Thus, each of us must continually translate what "I" think I know into knowledge that we think "we" know. To the extent that this translation is successful, it both enables us to communicate better with each other and becomes that which we in fact know that we know.

What came into the LC as personally differentiated and/or individually held knowledge is, therefore, transformed into either socially known and/or collectively shared knowledge. This form of knowledge is not necessarily any "truer" in an epistemological sense. It is, however, possibly more efficacious, since it provides a dynamic possibly informing collective action.

It is also, then, a context in which remaining, personally-differentiated knowledge is transformed itself into self-consciously known as different and self-consciously held as different, with some recognition of how and why it is different from that held by others. There emerges a second level of socially real shared knowledge: the shared sense of how and why persons continue to differ in what they take to be the state of the world or some aspect of that world, material or mental.

By the mere praxis of LCP, participants also learn that the process by which they enrich their personal view of the world and themselves is the very process by which others do the same. Out of such realization, there hopefully comes a commitment to open processes of learning and eloquence—dynamics that also build community as well as feed the incipient sense of a newly emerging community, which originally underwrote participants' trust, humility, and love of each other and of learning that enhances itself.

Such shared knowing becomes knowledge in a socially real sense. It can then become the basis for shared action to achieve common goals. LCP enables participants to translate personal knowledge, which, as such, is socially inert, into personally held social knowledge, which, to that degree, becomes socially efficacious. "What do I know?" and "What am I to do?" are translated into "What do *we* know?" and "What are *we* to do?"

Meditation X: Pedagogical Reversals in a Learning Community

The emerging primacy of efficacious knowledge within a community of learners, then, poses a paradoxical task to the teacher-as-learner. One way to highlight this paradox is by reference to the typical refrain addressed to a primary skill needed by the seminar "teacher," who is presumably the "leader" of a seminar discussion. For example, an everpresent dictum among educators has it that "To teach a seminar class, you must learn how to *lead* a discussion."

LCP suggests an inversion of this principle. Rather than leading a discussion, the issue becomes: "To participate as a teacher/learner in a Learning Community, you must learn how to *follow* a discussion." Professorial leadership becomes a kind of informed followership. The agenda of LCP is student driven; but an alertly-following professor may help steer the discussion, not to *apriori* important points, professorial priorities, or "planned interpretations," but to perennial human themes and current embodiments, so that students derive a sense of being more fully human—following the noble quest of knowingly surviving and seeking authentic dignity within an inclusivist vocation as a species carrier.

Following a discussion requires actively-focused listening. LCP listening is more akin to hearkening, that is, active participatory listening, not mere passive receptive hearing. Anyone with ears can hear. Only focused ears, head, and heart can hearken to what students are saying. The meat of what any of us "says" is in what is not said—perhaps cannot even be said; and it almost certainly lies beyond the cognitive reach of the speaker at that moment of speech/thinking/risk taking, when self puts self's assertions and limitations into a shared arena as a public object, for the critical responses of others.

Leading a discussion implies that there is a known goal or object of knowledge to the discussion; an efficacious means for arriving at that cognitive object; and that learners are judged by their adherence to the means and their assimilation of the object. Following a discussion, by contrast, suggests that there is no *apriori* known object of knowledge to be sought by all participants; that the efficacious means are wide ranging and include whatever enlightens the minds, fires the hearts, and joins the understandings of the participants; and that participants are to be judged both by what they come to understand and by their own awareness that they have taken possession of that which they understand, out of their own connatural and interactional resources, which are, thus, incipiently universal.

A primary pedagogical outcome of following a discussion is to help students articulate what they are incipiently thinking and feeling sufficiently, to motivate them to speak and construct an object for others' responses. This is risky self-exposure, and students react differently according to their risk-taking capabilities; hence, the challenge of the shy student who may rarely take the risk. The teacher-learner strives to follow in this midwife sense: following up on the cognitive contractions to give birth to the student-participants' thoughts. A concept is the fruit of students' cognitive conceiving. The teacher-learner is the midwife who offers encouragement and, indeed, acts encouragingly.

The teacher-learner, then, helps at the same time to give birth to the LC's culture: Instead of a student feeling and appearing stupid or inarticulate or incoherent, in the judgmental eyes of leaders of discussions and of other participants, the right of the student to speak elicits the duty of others to help the student realize what she or he is trying to conceive and say. The more confused the attempt, the more material for the group to create and clarify. Indeed, I recall a sociologist, C. Wright Mills, saying that in one's confused thinking and speaking lie the seeds of one's creative ideas. Confusion manifests a potentially creative moment. As a community, we are all involved in thinking/learning; and our culture tells us to see behind and beyond the mere words of the speaker into the assumptions and worldview from which those utterances originate, what they may mean to hearers, and how they are thus reflected back to the speaker.

Following rather than leading a discussion is but one of a family of reversals that a Learning Community professor learns to enact. Consider the imperative that the professor must be an "expert." The professor presumably knows all that is relevant to the issues and is able to answer all questions. Above all else, the professor must not appear to be ignorant in the face of sharp student questioning. LCP reverses this know-it-all imperative. The professor may be an expert in some specialty, but no human is an expert in what really confronts all humans. Expert is a functionary; professor is an educator. Functionaries apply the rationality and data bases of institutional logics. Educators empower students to learn, and to learn how to learn, and in so doing generate efficacious knowledge with others committed to cooperative action, to render the species sustainable.

The expert role is intermittently relevant to LCP, and the expert may or may not be the professor. Indeed, were the professor to claim the role of expert, that very claim would transform student participants into nonexperts. This is another version of role-identities that are part of the "black box" model of abstracted teaching—as the downloading of information from the head of the professor into the heads of students, which is a process akin to transferring bytes of info within cyberspace.

Since the contexts for topics are shared problems and perennial issues, no one is an expert in all relevant aspects. Student participants, therefore, may be more expert than the professor, especially when discussing the "texts" of students' own experiences. The Learning Community as a community is the final resource—read "expert"—since expertise is specialized knowledge, whereas problem-issues apply specialized knowledge to a range of value hierarchies, policy options, and action imperatives toward sustainability. Professors in LCP redefine expertness as a resource that all communities need and which they seek as needed.

As potential experts themselves, then, students avoid the dualistic opposition identities of "nonexpert" or "ignorant," which are interactionally imposed on them, if the professor proclaims self as the only expert, and makes that proffered identity the core of the professorial relationship with students. Such a claim and oppositional imposition of identities also renders students as "powerless," since in an intellectual domain, knowledge, learning, expertise, information, etc. are sources of power. The degree to which a professor claims an expert identity is the degree to which a professor renders students powerless.

These dynamics fall under a conventional pedagogical principle for the teacher: Keep control! LCP reverses this principle: Give control! Control as an empirical dynamic in a Learning Community shifts to the group dynamics and the self-realization of participants. The professor remains as a sort of "helmsperson" who is not captain of the ship, but, rather, guide and cultural broker—a kind of normative midwife to help the group generate a little society and emergent group subculture that may generate critical and shared learning.

Authority, then, passes from the professor to the group. If it emerges as legitimate in the awareness of participants, then the shared authority generates concomitant shared responsibility, duties, and mutual bestowal of rights to speak, challenge, support and be supported, and search for efficacious knowledge in safe space and time. The channeling effect of authority as a defining aspect of what is truth, what is worth asking, what is worth learning, who is worthy of asking or responding, whose experience is relevant or valid, who puts final closure on an issue—all these authoritative dimensions of the process of learning are experienced in the group itself, not imposed from an external authority, an *apriori* framework, or a privileged set of past conventional answers. Removing this legitimating retrospective and *apriori* authority opens the group to learning, in terms of emerging presents and possible futures—futures that will then make demands on such thinkers/students to pursue the best empirical and causal knowledge that is relevant to the futures they are beginning to imagine.

To put this issue metaphorically, until the learning community kills the professor role, participants will not learn! Authority emerges as intrinsic to the learning process itself, along with the criteria of criticism that monitors all that participants are willing to accept as knowledge of the world. Recall the principle formula informing this version of LCP: eloquence expressing critical intelligence in pursuit of universal human values. The authority generated within the group, in a word, remains self-critical and open to ever-contingent reformulations of future worlds. Such critical authority, then, arises from the sources of knowledge and experience that the LC is able to marshal. One ancient epistemological ground for truth, the witness of experience—"*teste experientia*"—enters participants' awareness as they present, hear, and weigh experiences shared as members of a Learning Community, and attribute appropriate truth claims arising from recognition of each others' legitimate real-world experiences. And it quickly becomes apparent that student participants have experiences relevant to the perennial issues that arise, experiences that at appropriate junctures are recognized as much more relevant to contemporary patterns and likely futures than those of the professor, especially a professor as far from them in age as the present writer, who predates student lives by more than three generations!

Given a stock of shared experiences, vicarious and actual, the LC has real-life materials for intellectual and rational discussion that take the readings and prescribed pedagogical matters out of academic space and locate or at least apply them in experiential contexts. Perennial issues and relevant empirical patterns and causal interpretations take on new life and verisimilitude, within the now-shared experiences in which they are realized.

Another convention sometimes attributed to teaching is to "give the answer to a question." LCP, on the other hand, suggests questions to all answers. Questions survive—indeed they are perennial challenges to human survival. Answers come and go with the exigencies, problems, knowledge, and technological knowhow of the age. As soon as an answer is implemented, new issues inevitably arise that elicit the same perennial questions, which then elicit another generation of contingent and necessarily ephemeral answers—as phenomenologists might say, "for the time being." What am I to do? is a question that survives from the Adam-Eve dynamic in "Genesis" or the Arjuna-Krishna dialogue in the *Bhagavad Gita*. And that same question informs the lives and decisions of students and professors day in and day out, as it must, *per saecula saeculorum*, throughout the ages.

The professor, then, eschews sole claim to expertness, and, indeed, thematizes expertness as a handmaiden to community issue-defining procedures and actional imperatives aroused by reasking the perennial questions. In the spirit of Socrates, in an LCP, the professor may claim only that wisdom which Socrates claimed for himself, even after being named by the Delphic Oracle as the wisest person in Athens. After conversing with and discerning a statesman's wisdom, Socrates concludes, "Neither of us knows anything beautiful and good, but he thinks he does know when he doesn't, and I don't know and don't think I do: so I am wiser than he is by only this trifle, that what I do not know I don't think I do" (quoted in *Great Dialogues of Plato*, p. 427. Mentor Books, 1956).

LCP builds momentum out of recognition of gaps in knowledge, the absence of absolute certitude, and overgeneralized expertness. This ground-up or *aposteriori* participatory pedagogy implicates another reversal of a sometime teaching convention—teachers transmit knowledge. As I overheard a student commenting to another student about some class, "I knew more about it than the teacher!" At other times, students may well be more versed on the Web and Internet resources, which have attained a range of authenticity from the fraudulent to the legitimate, with various special interests spread across that range. The teacher, in other words, may or may not be a black box full of more data, history, science, policy options, and actual experience than students in any domain that revolves around perennial issues and outside the autogenerating knowledge of disciplinary matrices relatively unknown to students.

So the convention to "transmit knowledge" reintroduces issues of What is knowledge? What is relevant? What is the cognitive payoff of experience? Why is older more knowledgeable than younger? If the present is a set of crises, and if past understandings generated the crises, why should participants believe that knowledge from the past will temporarily resolve the problems and address the issues that past understandings either generated or exacerbated? Good questions, all.

To respond to these unanswerable questions and to supplement the convention to transmit knowledge, I work toward what is a more basic grounding of learning, namely, to try and elicit wonder. If a pedagogy generates wonder, then students need a space and time with the freedom to pursue their wonder-ful responses to satisfy that wonder, which works like an appetite for the true and the good, as best they can discern these philosophical transcendentals in their wonder. Students then seek relevant knowledge as the goal of their intrinsic sense of autonomous energy and cognitive journey.

Professors, then, do not provide answers from the past, only past answers. The emergent contexts of students' futures require application of any answers to the ever-renewed questions generated by students' new-felt wonder. In a basic sense, the past provides stronger causal accounts for present crises rather than for causal likelihood of escaping these crises. After all, present crises result from past ways of thinking and resultant actions. How, then, can reapplication of past thinking answer the crises those very thought patterns and actions brought upon us?

Wonder at possible futures informs socially efficacious learning in every sense of social: generated by social interaction among learners in the search for shared understandings and values that have a chance to motivate cooperative collective action toward sustainable living. Answers are proleptic; they lie in the projected futures and shared risks to attain futures, in which all learners have a fair likelihood of pursuing their well being. And, of course, those futures forever recede and must be reprojected in the inherent human task of sharing proleptically in wonderful possibilities of shared futures.

Answers, then, are ephemeral, incomplete, provisional, and, as follows necessarily from the irony and pathos of collective action, carry their own probabilities of added risks, threats, and negative outcomes. As one of the principles of folk "ecolacy," or the ability to read environmental meanings akin to literacy or numeracy, has it, "There are no free lunches," from human intervention into ecological dynamics. Every intervention to attain a positive outcome necessarily includes additional outcomes, and one or more of them are likely undesirable if not downright threatening. This is an ecological application of the now-understood principle of contemporary technological society's causal posture as paradoxically a "risk" society. Risk society members reflexively understand that, in the very actions of producing socially defined goods, they necessarily also produce environmentally and, eventually, socially understood "bads." Progress in areas A, B, etc. spells regress in areas Sub A, Sub B, etc. The automobiles and other internal combustion engine vehicles provide welcome locomotion and hauling of products. They also provide polluted air, soil, and water; loss of habitat and arable soil; gridlock; and social noise pollution, which threaten residential areas, not to mention roughly 30,000 traffic deaths annually in the United States—a staggering number of deaths that appear normal, unavoidable, and noncontroversial compared to, I suggest, any other source of even one-tenth that many corpses!

Given current teaching-learning practices and the use to which they are put by educational institutions and taken over by post-baccalaureate enterprises such as business corporations, to make judgments about students-as-employees, conventional definitions tell us that grades measure learning. What is hidden in this assumption is that grades also transform learning and teaching, as we discuss below. Rather than grades measuring learning in a LC sense, learning generates the kind of evaluation that is appropriate to that mode of learning. In a real sense, then, learning measures grades as a social construct. Grades as institutional objectifications appropriated by corporate or governmental America do not automatically or uncritically measure learning in a sense relevant to LCP.

Rather, as extrinsic to the learning-teaching dynamic, grades take on a function and standing as indicators of reward and punishment for students' conformity to teachers' performance expectations. As such, grades become tools for corporate or governmental consumers of students' post-graduation lives. Grades are part of a pedagogy that assumes that, in order for students to learn, they must be behaviorally modified by rewards and punishments and driven by such extrinsic followups. Such an approach to the good of student evaluation transforms evaluation and the teacher-student relationship into one of external, tradable, commodified reification of that good. Such transformation, furthermore, defines students and the learning they are experiencing as an external constraint and students become vulnerable to punishments-rewards, like any other behaviorally modified animal. Finally, such double transformations threaten to transmogrify learning from an evolutionarily selected intrinsically satisfying experience to a socially defined extrinsically cost-benefit chit.

Granted that there are, in principle, institutionally justified contexts and training demands that reasonably call for extrinsic grading and black-box pedagogy, there are risks such as control rather than empowerment attached to that dynamic as to any pedagogy. LCP tries to work with evolutionary and practical problem-solving and shared cooperative knowledge aspects of learning, and thus go beyond institutionalized third-party ratings of the teacher-learner relationship. Pragmatically speaking, a core aspect of learning is that it is pleasurable and meaningful. It is an evolutionary advantage with both species and personal outcomes. Grades and the processes for generating them must at times reflect these intrinsic core aspects.

Meditation XI: Learning Community Pedagogy And Temporary Answers

Answers, temporary though they are, come, as it were, from outside of the individual. In social terms, humans act upon their surroundings and each other in institutional patterns that follow a social rationality, which may or may not be rational for individuals or their relationships with physical environments or their emerging futures. In brief, institutions are constructed and maintained by humans, who in some sense are individuals, but institutions also have outcomes that no individual intends and may not even foresee. No individual commuter intends to add to the likelihood that his children may develop asthma or breast cancer, yet the very act of driving may well have some measurable or hypothetical link to such unintended and unwanted outcomes. Such is a dawning, gradually confronted, contemporary extension of the inherent irony of human action, namely, in acting to achieve a good, I may also attain a bad.

Efficacious learning, as understood here, occurs only in a social matrix, involves proleptic futures, and finds institutional or social movement enactments. Collective action based on efficacious learning is always in terms of an implicated future and never a certitudinous application of *apriori* or univocal from-the-past answers; and it remains only "for the time being," since in the very enactment, it generates new issues.

Efficacious learning in a LCP is a type of shared intellect that differs from conventional understandings of rationality, ideology, or faith. Rationality, in this sense, incorporates a means-end reductionism. It refers to the purposive rationality attributed to contemporary rational choosers acting within a capitalist-cultural hegemony. A longer tradition supplements this means-end reductionistic rationality, by emphasizing that there is no means-end schema that can dictate ultimate or final "ends," if, indeed, they are irreducible to their means. This reductionist rationality, then, is a handmaiden to often-unexamined nonrational or, at least, arational, ends, which emerge from persons' and groups' value commitments. LCP dynamics help learners discover, articulate, take responsibility for, and adjust their values to those of others, and hopefully, for all to learn how to incorporate what is universal and inclusive in their values with the same scope as found in others' values.

LCP also unmasks learners' ideologies, or often-unselfconscious and occasionally aggressively-conscious worldviews and legitimating myths, which knowingly or not serve their personal or group interests against those of others. Ideology is difficult to unmask, precisely because it is the cultural *existenz* or social air we each breathe, so that it too often remains transparently invisible to each of us, like air is to mammals' vision, and perhaps water to fish's eyes. Ideas in the service of interests at least can be made self-conscious and subjected to a calculus of competing interests and their legitimating ideologies, as long as these are linked to empirical outcomes and at-hand experiences.

Faith, as belief in transcendental objects, persons, or dynamics, in contrast to ideology, lies beyond the reach of generalizable practical interests and empirical outcomes. In this sense, it is forever unfalsifiable and derives its accent of reality from the act of handing over one's personal judgment to that of an outside sacred authority. I take faith as the location of judgment and existential posting of things, symbols, and forces into the mind or judgment of an other. In the case of sacred faith in a *totaliter aliter* of a Divine Other, the loss of autonomy is ultimate, certain, and taken-as-truth about the world, its inhabitants, and their respective futures. Such faith may lie outside of LCP and its emergent, experiential, and empirical groundings.

On a lower frequency than sacred faith, both *apriori* rationality and legitimating ideologies stand in opposition to LCP. LCP is grounded in a pragmatic and universal evolutionary capability shared, in some degree, by all members of the human family; that is what I intend by the term—intelligence as the acting out of an assumed capability referenced as intellect. Intellect, though the hardware, as it were, that is housed in each individual's skull, much like the hardware in each person's PC, is a shared and social cognitive capability, much as the software and knowledge domain "existing" in the shared social space of cyber knowledge.

The kind of efficacious learning that is a primary goal of LCP is a constant interaction between what the individual learner experiences as personal and what the group, sharing adjustments, enacts as shared and, thus, supportive of a likelihood of underwriting collective cooperative action toward common issues. In this pragmatic sense, then, intellect is efficaciously social and not individual, though, to be sure, the individual must both learn what others in the group come to know and adjust, perhaps even compromise, in the many cognitive and affective nuances of that term, so that the community may address common issues. LCP informs a social matrix of shared interactive learning-teaching that informs probabilities that cooperative action will result. Such shared, interactive, learning-teaching manifests what I take to be evolutionary intelligence: species potential for collective solving of shared problems, always only for the time being.

Evolutionary intelligence is a capacity shared by all humans. It is also a capacity that is overlaid with cultural constraints and interpretive schema, which restrict its application and historically exclude outsiders from its dynamics. Evolutionary intelligence is inclusive, universal, and adaptive for future possibilities. Cultural rationalities, ideological commitments, and faith conformities are exclusive, particularistic, and repetitive from past conventions. Evolutionary intelligence is a key capacity for species adaptation; and given the critical problems facing the current generation—through cultural conflict, new local warfare, environmental threats, and spread of weapons of mass destruction—not only adaptation but sustainability and, perhaps, survival in any current understanding of that state of being is profoundly at risk. The defining issues for LCP revolve around basics such as air, soil, water, food, energy, identity, culture, meaning, violence, inclusivity, and cooperation that go beyond the definitional reach and methodological assumptions of regnant cultural versions of rationality, ideology, and faith.

Meditation XII: Learning Community Characteristics

Community, as a dynamic social reality, is at least an organization of persons sharing a time, space, and set of defining recurrent issues for survival. As such, community is always forming and re-forming itself in the face of issues for survival in its social surroundings and physical environment. This Meditation contains five aspects of a community geared to learning: shared origin and destiny; future orientation; social efficaciousness; scientific empiricalness; and democratic inclusivity.

First, community is grounded in a *shared sense of origin and destiny*. Many ask, How can this be? Obviously, there are multiple senses of different origins and irreconcilable destinies. The religions of the world codify these irreconcilable origins and destinies in their etiological myths and transcendent fates, as the Christian version of standing to the right or left "Hand of Divinity," as sheep or goats, in the eschatological scene that forever sends the saved and damned to their separate eternities. Historical traditions, geographical placements, symbolic cultural worlds, and discrete languages present us with the biblical Babel of peoples who do not indeed share a common language, sense of common origin, and destiny.

A sense of shared origin and destiny also trumps the excessive ontologization of the individual as a source of meaning and outcome. Individuals may compete with and against each other in delimited market and sporting arenas, but not in terms of that which unites us ultimately in the struggle to survive and sustain ourselves on this Earth, just as groups and societies need to subordinate their traditional interests to the shared environmental, moral, legal, social, and physical needs of all humans *qua* human, as well as *qua* animal.

Individuals and societies need to commit themselves to a prior communal understanding of what they share as humans interested in survival and sustainability, in order that they may formulate goals and means to strive for policy responses to perennial issues that generate our more delimited problems. LCP helps us all learn and communicate what we all must do if we all are to survive.

A primary imperative of a LC, then, is to elicit from participants just such a sense of shared origin and destiny. Indeed, this imperative is a counter to a sense of immediate crisis that fires LC dynamics in the first place. No matter what our empirical, social, cultural, and mythic differences, we need to discover what of our various origins and destinies we, in fact, share simply by our being human. LCP is based on a foundation of a pragmatic humanistic realization, a realization that demands that we see through all that separates us until we discern what unites us in common issues and this-worldly outcomes.

Second, community has a *future orientation*. The core dynamic of social survival in the face of perennial issues, through unending institutional problem-solving, makes community necessarily future oriented. Issues of survival are never solved once and for all. In application, communities respond to such issues as problems to be resolved for the time being. Institutional arrangements solve them for a time, often and increasingly generating wider distal problems as they work to solve delimited immediate ones. In a word, societal difficulties are not "problems" that have a certified "solution." They are "issues" that demand constant "adjustments."

In today's social reflection, contemporary First World societies are known as "risk societies," in the sense that we often create deeper problems as we solve more surface ones. Where that leaves us in relation to the perennial issues is the open question of sustainability. LCP, then, recognizes the paradox of risk creation in problem solving. Thus, everyone's voice in LCP must be heard to maximize the likelihood that as many aspects of the problem in relation to larger issues are taken into account, before the shared knowledge becomes efficacious policymaking to guide group reactions.

As our native-born philosophical pragmatism, adequately understood, would have it, society, as well as self, is ever adapting and reconstructing itself, if you allow a personification of society. Society, like self, is ever-emerging, even as it concerns itself with continuity and conservation, in a vital sense. Community dynamics are never-ending balancing processes of emergence, freedom, and creativity, interfacing with structure, continuity, restraint, and reproduction. So, too, LCP is laced with these tensions, but the primacy is with the former. In a LCP lemma, freedom is a central principle of a LC, and that includes recognition of both freedom *for* expression and freedom *from* punitive responses, including grading in some instances.

LCP rejects the illusion of stasis that confounds what is with what will be; the functionalist fallacy of equating what is with what is fittest; and the moralist reduction of equating what was with what is right. Genuine community, like society and self, is a process of continually addressing issues arising from surroundings and environment and readdressing the self and societal understanding that emerges from those encounters.

Third, as community addresses continuing issues of survival, it must ever seek *socially efficacious knowledge*. LCP highlights knowledge as a social production, possession, and instrument of survival. Such knowledge, however, must be socially efficacious as well. The most profound wisdom, the greatest scientific breakthrough, the most powerful technological application, the deepest radical social arrangement—as long as they remain individual actions and personal possessions, they will never become socially efficacious. It is in pragmatic adaptation that learning becomes our future.

Social applications, political or economic policies, collective actions, social movements, rebellions and revolutions, or surges of popular awareness are some of the social avenues through which learning becomes efficacious. Just so, LCP includes a dynamic for "socializing" learning, for taking it out of our subjective awareness, personal opinions, individualistic profit maximizing, and for learning not only to learn but to share learning with an eye toward enhancing community life and well being. Socially efficacious knowledge is interactionally realizable through cooperative collective action that addresses emergent problems linked to perennial issues.

Fourth, as an empirical and experiential undertaking in the most literal sense, communities are ways of living that depend on the best *empirical description* of the world and the best available *scientific understandings* of how the world works, to guide them in the types of collective actions they address, to solve problems arising from perennial issues, such as sustainable peace, air, water, soil, energy, and safe travel. Empirical, scientific, and technological feasibility and desirability open as profound sets of learning issues that become rapidly more complex, recursive, interdependent, and insoluble in any definitive sense, even as the necessity for acting becomes even more immediate.

Think, for example, of a presidential signing of the go-ahead for storing high-level nuclear leftovers in Yucca Mountain. Everyone agrees something must be done quickly; no one knows for sure what is best for everyone; and pure science and technology cannot solve the problem, while the topmost political and scientific actors disagree on how to address the issue of energy sources sufficient to power the way of life we are generating. This primary analogue of paradoxical issues points to the need for adequate empirical-scientific-technological knowledge that informs the socio-learning communities that decide policies and staff collective actions.

Students, as citizen-consumers of specialized knowledge mediated through lay channels, need to learn to learn what is known and what is taken on faith, among institutional knowledge producers. As consumers of knowledge, we are always dependent on the competence and honesty of the producers of knowledge. A key decision, then, is our community decision-making to invest our secular faith in one or another source of empirical descriptions of the world and scientific understandings of the dynamics of that world. Thus, we generate community policy based on our investing secular faith in this or that knowledge-producing institution or group.

The dynamic of discovering and articulating secular faith in cooperative policy formation or moral ways of living together brings us to the fifth feature of our Learning Community: It is *democratic* with a small d. Democratic community means that all participate in ways relevant to what they share with others and what they contribute to the issues generating the problems that require attention. Democratic process is a continual readjustment between structure and tradition, process and future. Present re-adjustments implicate reconstructions of what futures we foresee in our collective lives.

As a pluralistic, democratic community, it is structurally and processually contrasted with religious fundamentalisms and ideological certitudes and reductionisms. Democratic community life focuses on responding to shared problems of living into shared futures. Transcendental destinies from mythopoeic revelations or certitudinous presents, derived from *apriori* political or economic ideologies, are now subordinated to this-worldly concerns with air, water, soil, energy, peace, social identities, and personal dignity. Democratic communities strive to eliminate misery and degrading inequality—a deeper issue than material poverty that, in itself, does not necessarily threaten physical life and social dignity.

The final step is professorial contributions to democratic LC formation. At the end of the session and at opportune moments during discussion—moments for which there are no *apriori* or fixed times—a professor-as-teacher may contribute the following learning aspects: articulate unstated values and principles and logics underlying participants' contributions to the discussion; summarize synthesizing themes that began to emerge from the discussion as a whole; ennoble the themes by linking them with perennial and classical versions of these same themes, showing that today's concerns are not unique to today and that felt risks and anxieties may well be part of the noble vocation of humans throughout history; and suggest challenges to ways of living, personally and collectively, arising out of the themes that students themselves generated in their discussions. To face the problems arising from perennial issues reconstructed here and now has been forever a grounding dimension of human nobility. Students and professors live out totally human vocations in their participation in an LC. It is what humans have always done and must always continue to do until there is no community left on earth.

Meditation XIII: Unlearning Conventions to Unleash a Learning Community

Experience with LCP brought this professor to relearn teaching, and in so doing, to unlearn standard conventions. Consider the following conventional underlying assumption: Knowledge maketh a bloody entry so that learning is difficult, painful, stressful, disciplined, standardized, and routinized, so that the same rules and procedures apply to everyone. A corollary of this assumption is that the professor must do the following: quiz, pop-quiz, test, examine, and relentlessly grade, discipline, and extrinsically motivate students—or they will not learn. Such an educational philosophy seems based on an assumption that learning is somehow unnatural and externally imposed, so that standardized institutional arrangements of rewards and punishments are necessary to motivate students to learn. A corollary of this philosophy is that students need to learn in a style, manner, and mode according to a schedule, timetable, and endpoint imposed by the batch-processing rationalities of classes, semesters, years, requirements, and extrinsically applied rules.

At times, it appears that an adversarial dynamic emerges in which students are recalcitrant, almost antagonistic enemies to the professor's "enterprise"—and this business-derived word is used advisedly in the current university atmosphere. On the contrary, a professor may assume that learning is a natural process, inherently pleasurable, and intrinsically motivating. Learning is as naturally pleasurable as a slurpy or ice-cream soda on a hot summer midday. The natural pleasure is an immediate outcome of the essential human being as an "animal rationale," or rational animal, for whom acting out rationality is intrinsically pleasurable—or so LCP assumes.

On the basis of this assumption, the following canards of pedagogy evoke reexamination:

1. Teaching is a "performing art" and the professor is "on," as the unifocused star of the performance.

2. The professor is the authority, and such authority derives from expert knowledge that exceeds the knowledge or—as one sometimes hears—ignorance of students.

3. The professor realizes his or her authority by exercising power and controlling the class.

4. The professor legitimates control by knowing all the answers or claiming to be able to find the answers.

5. The professor decides what is important to learn.

6. The professor structures the tempo, content, format, identities, and roles of and for the actors.

7. The professor predefines what outcomes are valued and what objectives justify those outcomes.

8. Teaching success is measured by the amount of #7 the students can be shown to have assimilated and can reproduce within the timeframe structured into the class and so-called examination periods, instead of allowing students to take examinations when they are ready for them.

9. Learning, then, is defined as the outcome of the *apriori* characteristics of the teaching content and dynamics, so that learning is discrete, objective, testable, and measurable: What is learned is that which is reproduced in examinations. Though there is a timeframe for teaching, there is no timeframe for learning; in a word, learning is said to be demonstrated at the moment of taking the examination, with no reckoning of the duration of that which is examined and perhaps forgotten tomorrow.

10. Students' personal experiences are irrelevant to content and dynamics of the course, and at times, an obstacle to *apriori* teaching objectives.

11. Professors predefine or vet all students' actions and presentations in class.

12. Professors realize their authority and control by grading, appearing to grade, or spot- grading every action, task, statement, assignment, and presence in class. There are no time outs, especially for sleeping.

Within professorial culture, one occasionally or more often hears indications of teaching and the absence of learning in socially acceptable "of course" statements, some of them used in the quasiofficial language of departmental and higher administrative discourse. Consider the following:

1. Teaching is a "load," as in such language as "The regular teaching load for regular faculty is two courses per semester." Questions arise as to the cultural contents, evaluations, and meanings of the "load." Luckily, Professor A has a "light teaching load" this semester.

2. Teaching is a commodity that can be "bought off." Professor B bought off one course per semester with an outside research grant.

3. Teaching is time from which one can be "released." Professor C has released time from teaching in order to undertake other work. Professors, prisoners, and patients get released time from obligations.

4. Professors are to be happy when students leave at the end of the semester, especially in May, and sad when students return for the start of classes in the fall, as reflected in too- typically rueful hallway exchanges among faculty.

5. Professors are thought to prefer writing, submitting grants, reading, attending conferences, or consulting, rather than teaching. Indeed, promotion and tenure committees are reported to have warned young untenured or not-yet-renewed faculty that they ought not spend so much time with students. Such committee cultures reflect institutional priorities reflected in the scuttlebutt saying, "Good teaching will never get you tenure, but bad teaching may get you axed."

These are some of the stock-in-trade principles a professor has learned to unlearn. It is not clear what that professor may have learned instead.

Meditation XIV: Rethinking Grading Practices For a Learning Community

LCP brings a professor to certain new understandings that depart from the ways he or she may have been socialized into thinking about good teaching practices. Learn to beware the ubiquitous positivist fallacy "Only that is knowable which is measured," and its corollary "Measurement generates knowledge." This fallacy leads to Grade Point Averages with numbers carried to the third or more decimal point to decide rankings. Rankings and numbers supposedly measure what the student learned. These numbers are generated by taking tests prepared by someone else and translating responses into digits or letters, and each of these can be translated back again.

Tests and examinations are, however, heteronomous definitions of learning and of the outcomes of teacher-student interaction, as well as of the students' activities of reading, reflecting, writing, deciding, feeling, stressing, physically ailing or well fit, responding to family relationships and the concomitant fates of their kinfolk. Tests externalize learning into what is either in the exam maker's head or in standardized test banks. Testing is too often measurement of black-box learning: What is in the teacher's head or sources must get into the head of the student, and then that content must be externalized and measured. Testing as measurement of learning transforms education for learning into teaching for tests.

Key questions arise: What learning is tested? How efficient are tests at measuring what is tested? Etcetera. The testing industry of American education attests to these issues. From a LCP perspective, testing is a reduction and transmogrification of learning—necessary for certain purposes, usually institutional ones, but not coextensive with learning.

Given these constrictions from testing, LCP tries to wean students from examinations and tests as intrinsic indicators of learning. This is not a simple process. Some students so internalize institutionalized measures of successful learning that they protest the lack of tests. Others become upset at one LCP professor's refusal to make comments on exams, although he comments on students' papers that they write about their chosen topics.

A premise of this Meditation is that LCP is corrupted by "scores," and the greatest of these are "grades." From a social-psychological perspective, grades may, indeed, measure some aspect of overall intelligence, and more likely some aspect of acquired information and vocabulary usage. In addition, however, grades measure behavioral and attitudinal conformity to authority and institutional imperatives built into school systems and classroom practices. Grades measure what was in the teacher's head or the curriculum designer's outcome objectives. Teaching plans generate grading strategies and tactics by both teachers and students. Such tactics and strategies are extrinsic to the learning-teaching processes themselves.

In addition, depending on the reference group informing a students' self understanding, grades may measure social desirability—either positively, if the student belongs to groups aligned with the teaching culture, or negatively, if the student defines self in relation to a group at odds with the learning/teaching culture of the school; this is a predicament for some individuals within social minorities that define good grades as selling out to the establishment. Such wrongs may even be righted via violence directed against the administration and other students. Grades become another rather public appearance through which one's identity is announced and responses to self's presence elicited for good or ill.

Once so publically announced, grades work like a generalized positional medium of exchange between the student and future markets, educational and occupational. Educational labor measured in grades is exchanged for occupational opportunity in the worlds of corporate careers or post-baccalaureate studies. Grades become a currency, a symbolic medium of exchange, an ersatz money for purchasing future opportunities. No good grades, no interview; no interview, no job. Besides asking how did learning get to become a currency, we need to reflect on what may be the implications for LC formation?

For a start, the transformation of learning outcomes into grades as a generalized medium of exchange between classroom and workplace violates the LC professional relationship between professor and student. The violation occurs in two sets of relationships. First, public exchange of grades transforms learning into scoring, and students then into competitive, often stressed, zero-sum players in an extrinsically-scored game, in which good grades are made into scarce goods that measure both what the student has measurably learned and what the student is publically worth.

Consider that we do not so translate health diagnoses, understandings, and evaluations between doctors and patients, nor legal diagnoses, communications, and judgments between lawyers and clients in exchangeable chits for the occupational or public world. We may add other professional relationships governed by norms of mutual disclosure and shared confidentiality, such as accountants, psychologists, and, paradigmatically, the religious confessor—strictly observed and even with legal standing in the case of sacramental confession between sinner and priest. These evaluative interactions are protected by professional confidentiality and even secrecy, although the general weakening of the professional ethos, and the marketable translation of all judgments about individuals, is breaking down the last walls of personal privacy. In a totally commodified exchange arena, personal privacy is a nonnegotiable construct, and thus under pressure to become negotiable, even to the extent of genetic codes, DNA testing, and likely occupational, marital, and insurance availability.

At any rate, LCP suggests that professor-student confidentiality is a professional commitment and should cover grades, which are a professor's scholastic evaluation and implicated diagnoses of students. If corporate and professional America wants to measure, compare, make predictions, and assess likely occupational opportunity or educational achievement, then let them construct, finance, and administer their own tests and not corrupt LCP professor-student relationships with exogenous risks, life chances, and career stressors. It is the confounding of evaluation of learning with the distribution and publication of grades that add false pressure to the learning moment. Grades as currently institutionalized channel and transform learning from an intrinsically enjoyable and totally human experience of intellectual and moral development and student growth into an extrinsic score that is linked to public standing in the eyes of authoritative others. As now often practiced, grading is a form of pollution within a LCP.

Meditation XV: LCP Within a Religiously Identified University

The openness and futurity of LCP poses a challenge to a university that founds itself on a distinctive collective identity grounded in a separate historical tradition. Yes, a university may claim that it is a university made distinctive by its origin within and maintenance of a "religious identity," though there are many colleges and universities identified within that tradition writ large.

LCP calls participants to go beyond all identities that are exclusivist and divisive. Religious identities are such by design and definition, in part because they apotheosize an empirical past. Not everyone shares that same past and thus they are likely to be excluded from either a this-worldly or other-worldly transcendent future. University identities, on the other hand, are inclusivist and universalizing by design and definition, in part because they struggle to realize this-worldly empirical futures that in principle, and increasingly in fact, are in a globalizing economy and environmental context that include all of us.

A religious identity presents a challenge to LCP analogous to that posed by any prior exclusivist tradition, and most humans are born into such communities. The events of 9/11 and conflicts such as Israel/Palestine, Hindu/Muslim, Orange/Green Irish suggest the extremes to which the exclusivism of religious communities may bring us. Instances of religious-encompassed Learning Communities are also illustrated in the indoctrination and catechesis that preaches exclusivity, even to the extent of hatred toward other religions and, at times, the duty to kill infidels—norms that inform so-called universalist religions. So religious identity is transformed within LCP into a piece within a universalist experience of love of learning and love for one another among students.

Meditation XVI: Learning as an Evolutionary Community Process

The "best bet" for human pedagogy is an evolutionary perspective driven by universally shared intellect: a hopeful pragmatic quest working for a more sustainable, peaceful, and fair future community. Learning is a definitive animal response to environments, a response involving sets of adaptations to and interventions with physical, social, and moral environments.

From a pragmatic perspective, such interactional responses are aimed at the future and not the past. Assimilating and communicating the past is pragmatically relevant to the extent that it enables individuals to live and act as sustaining community members in the present. Pragmatic learning is not mere antiquarianism, a love for the past as past. Rather, it is reconstituted antiquarian understandings fitted to today's issues.

As stated in other terms above, learning relevant to LCP derives from intellect, from individuals communicating and interacting in pursuit of shared intelligence, and from mutual efficacious knowledge applicable to personal fulfillment and social sustainability for the common good. Learners realize intelligence as efficacious knowledge generated by what we may think of as social intelligence. Social intelligence is a type of efficacious knowledge that emerges from interactive processes of mutual realization, which characterize collectively defined issues and implicate community problem solving. Cooperative action and teamwork follow from social intelligence applied to shared issues and challenges, problems, and enacted values, such as fairness, security, peace, and sustainability.

Mere rational "problem solving" is part of social intelligence, but not the source of its dynamism and relevance. Problem solving refers to shortterm, particularistic actions that remain within larger issue and value-oriented coping, with the obligation to endure as a species. Problem solving is intelligence "here and now" and "for the time being." What remains foundational is the necessity of locating problems within larger issues that face us as a species. Thus, rational problem solving occurs within a context of shared learning and social intelligence that enables us not only to solve problems but to redefine them as well. In a word, we must learn how to think and act toward valued issues as a context for learning how temporally to solve this or that particular problem.

We may believe that problems are solved, but we know now that issues and values never are solved once and for all. Thus, answers to problems come and go, are correct and efficacious today but possibly wrongheaded and further endangering tomorrow. Dumping sewage and waste into the nation's waterways or burying radioactive waste in corrodible barrels was considered rational disposal yesterday. Today such dumpings are defined and regulated as acts of pollution, with waterways and soils already contaminated or threatened. Tomorrow, past dumpings must be cleaned up in hundreds of sites around the country, and waterways and foodways must be monitored and measured. So questions arise, even elementary questions, such as: How ought I and, *a fortiori*, we eat? How ought I and we dispose of my and our fecal waste and that of the hundreds of millions of animals? How may we all eat without threatening the waterways and foodways of our children? Kindred questions abound pointing to problems that were presumably solved yesterday but which are questioned anew today, to be solved yet again tomorrow and likely not yet permanently. To cooperate efficaciously in shared sustainable living, we must learn to learn together and act in concert.

Social intelligence goes beyond all identifiers and definitions that have divided the human species: idols of the tribe that serve to fire a reductionist belief in myths of one's nation or state; idols of the altar that motivate reductionist beliefs in divine favor bestowed upon "us" and disfavor visited upon "them;" and idols of ideology that rationalize beliefs in impersonal causal laws that rationalize humans taking shortterm profit above social equity.

Social intelligence is an intrinsic dynamic driving a liberal education. LCP enacts the freedom of thought and communication that makes thought, action, and existence liberal by freeing one's intellect from *apriori* conventions inherited from the past. The first move in liberal education is freedom *from* past received and posited transcendent understandings of what has gone on before and what ought to be done next. Understanding the current human condition as one of emerging crisis—a grounding premise of this type of LCP—demands freedom from *aprioris* of the past and transcendental posits of mythical futures. Put simply, those *aprioris* and posits generated the present species predicament and current critical juncture. They are not likely, then, to generate new and efficacious ways of being human and living with others and the environments we share.

Freedom *from* the *aprioris* of nostalgic pasts and posits of mythical futures clear space and time *for* the freedom generated by the emergence of empirical social intelligence. Contemporary forms of such liberal education include base communities in Latin America and elsewhere that enable participants to gain new voices expressing newly won awareness of the empirical truth of their situation, which had been masked by the received *aprioris* and posits of a repressive culture and institutional arrangements. The experience of Paolo Freire's *"consciousization"* by previously powerless peasants and illiterate workers is LCP at a critical juncture in their lives.

Social intelligence is oriented to knowledge implicated by shared images of desirable and mutual futures. Writ large, such shared images of mutual futures are species futures. Until our contemporary walk across the human stage, species futures were abstractions and philosophical efforts to cleanse and generalize our imaging and thinking. LCP in the two areas of involvement, human-environment and human-human relations, assumes that species futures are now empirical outcomes of current human activities in both social and physical realms.

Social intelligence, the overall knowing category of LCP, is always toward a future. As such, it is irreducible to *aprioris*, certainties, conventional meanings, and any kind of administered knowledge that preempts the necessity of humans to fashion sustainable futures through adequate shared understanding and doable cooperative action. These futures, then, are in the generic category of "utopian," in a technical not romantic understanding of that term. In this sense, utopian stands in opposition to "ideological," again in a technical sense, as that which finds functional truth from a posited past and tries to reenact that posited past, or myth, in today's circumstances—in a word, through a reactionary move to address future issues with past structures and privileges.

Social intelligence, then, is explicitly and logically and inherently value driven. Values are images of preferred futures. In this sense, they too are always contingent, not-yet, and hypothetical. Thus, they are front and center in what is taken as knowledge in LCP. It is in clarifying such futures that communities generate what we take as pragmatically true here and now, that is, as worthy of our agreement and cooperation.

Taking knowledge as sharing and cooperating for valued futures, and understanding learning as acquiring such interactional and relational knowledge, makes self-engagement with the pedagogical process a central dynamic of LCP. Futurity is a defining feature of human selfhood. These considerations lead us to renuance Descartes' lemma, "I think therefore I am," into "I think therefore I become"—or, better, "We think, therefore we become." The individual self realizes truth by participation in social learning within a community, and with internal dynamics ever to reach out to the most inclusive communities relevant to the issues at hand.

Such ever-widening reaching out for relevant Learning Communities point us in the direction of the young—thus the importance and increasing critical weight attached to appeals to evolutionarily universal capabilities of intelligence. Within the ethic of LCP, the young are entitled to this-worldly and empirically demonstrable sources of hope. LCP includes the charge to open intelligent communication that allows youth in interaction with the widest range of others to visualize preferred and possible futures that others prefer as well. Images of desirable futures are the stuff of hope, in this case, of this-worldly empirical pragmatic hope, not other-worldly transcendent mythic hope. Social learners, then, are able to participate in the intelligence that makes such desirable futures their own as well as others.

In brief, LCP dynamics bring participants toward ever more inclusivist identities and tasks. Social learning enacts the pluralism present in the identities and conventional truths that participants bring to the discussion. The enactment of participants' pluralism, however, may serve to divide members into exclusivist understandings and fall back into reactionary tribal or other *apriori* identities. Self-realization and display of the pluralism that is the human present, on the other hand, is a prelude to the possibility that all participants may see the potentiality and desirability of more inclusivist understandings of problems and more pointedly of one's self. Awareness of and active display of inclusivist identities and shared desirable futures configure communities' pluralities into reasons to share relevant understandings and cooperate for those desirable futures, without in any way eliminating that which makes each individual a self-referring person, and each tradition a self-legitimating source of particular meanings. Indeed, LCP drives participants to find the universal and inclusivist within the particularism and exclusivist historical meanings of their own experiences and traditions. It is akin to finding the universal spiritual meaning within each particular religious tradition and institutional logic.

Meditation XVII: Intergenerational Learning Communities and a Sense of History

One exercise I suggest to students is that they open lines of discussion with parents and grandparents about issues that arise in the LC. Such intergenerational discussions, especially if grandparents are included, give students a firsthand, face-to-face acquaintance with different biographic and familial experiences of central issues.

Salient issues often interpreted in different ways that students typically feel able to address are gender, race, sex, religion, environment, and national identity (especially for students from more recent immigrant families or minority backgrounds). The present student generation appears to be much more inclusive of traditionally excluded identities and the perception of the "other." Students comment on their differing attitudes toward gender roles over the three generations, typically with a traditional, domestic grandmother, a fulltime or parttime working or career mother, and their own expectations about how females will relate to potential husbands and how males will make their expectations clearer to potential wives.

In some cases involving the environment, grandparents cleared the land, perhaps broke the prairie, or recall tales of such pioneering tasks within their family traditions, whereas students may be inclined to value reconstruction of original ecosystems, such as wetlands, prairies, or woodlands now replaced by suburban housing developments. Indeed, in my environment course, one student from Iowa commented on the ambivalence he felt toward contemporary agribusiness and chemical-based farming, which lead to problems in soil communities and crop yields. In this context, he mentioned how his grandfather would comment emphatically about "those damn weeds" when they passed a restored prairie plot. The student totally understood his grandfather's attitude while experiencing his own ambivalence toward the dilemmas of agribusiness, suburban encroachment, and conflicts over legislation to restrict real estate speculation, subdivisions, and loss of prairie land to industrial farming.

Such intergenerational communication and awareness of historical changes lived within one's own family traditions is part of the learning that informs LCP. The "chickens" come home to roost in new ways, as these young people talk about how they define and whom they see as potential spouses. My classroom samplings point to a more inclusive identity acceptance among the students than their parents, and even more so than among their grandparents.

Meditation XVIII: Learning Community as Source and Context of Pedagogy

Community dynamics are intrinsic to realizing shared intellect. Intellect understood in this context is a species window to the world. Certitudinous ideologies, religious revelations, institutional rationalities, group interests, and cultural legitimations for power over others are all taken as opposed to social intellect. Intellect is what joins; all the others are what divide. Intellect informs learning that is future-oriented and thus open, *a posteriori*, contingent, hypothetical, and yet realizable and shareable—a delicate balance that requires constant rearranging and value sharing to become inclusive and universal.

Socially shared intellect through interaction with others generates emergent understandings that engage the individual's intellectual work and build social, emergent understandings. An emergent understanding combines parts of what participants brought with them to the discussion, some more than others. Communication among members of a LC is a generative process, driven by their love for learning and for each other. The three "motors" of interaction, communication, and emergent understandings are efficacious means toward the goods that genuine communities seek: peace, justice, security, sustainability, and acceptance.

The dynamic of shared intellect also has an ever-expanding reach: The boundaries of community must always be expanding to include those previously excluded. In this process of expanding inclusivity, the criteria of community membership and the types of love for others shift as well. Expanding the community to realize efficacious intellectual understanding in the face of shared issues does not mean the end of more traditional and exclusivist community membership experiences—a profound challenge to Earthlings' shared lives of personal understandings.

Universality is not corrosive of particularity but, rather, fulfills it in the context of emerging universal problems, and what we may think of as "hypergoods" made necessary and incipiently possible by ever-expanding material, social, financial, travel, environmental, and weapons-of-mass-destruction interdependencies. Universality makes the hypergoods of peace, justice, security, and sustainability possible. Our particular communities must, then, be subordinate to universal community ties that are relevant to those domains.

Learning Community Pedagogy based on generic interaction processes from which "teaching" and "learning" are abstractions both generates and emerges from an aborning Learning Community. Note the primacy of learning over teaching. The premise is that, as participants in the universal processes of intellect and critical learning, we are also teachers for self and each other.

Community arises from the trust that each has in the other and the relevance of the culture of the group for trustfully seeking shared goals. The group's small and temporary "community" incarnates a shared love for learning and for those in the community. Love here refers to the benevolent wishing and acting for each other's good that underwrites the common cultural good of the group. As an ancient adage has it, knowledge and thus learning is one of the common goods that can be shared and distributed ever more widely, without diminishing any individual's knowledge or learning. One thinks of peace and goodwill as other nondiminishing, common participatory goods. An LC arises from trust and engenders love for learning and one another.

Within an LC, the teacher is a "professor," one who has a sense of vocation derived from and, in turn, informing what the teacher "professes." To profess is to publically avow who one is, what one stands for, and what one is doing. In short, a professor professes a commitment to a common good within a universal intellectual quest to enhance the personal and common goods of others as student participants.

A paradox of LCP is that less professor talk often leads to more student learning. Professor talk dictates student assimilation. Professor silence opens space and time for student thinking and talking, at least for some. Silence is a key dynamic in LCP. Silence allows "Quaker moments" during which divinity or one's voiceless self may whisper and be heard, first by self and sometimes voiced for others to hear. The world would benefit from more silence, as institutionalized and mainly commercialized messages and cyber-sounds increasingly surround self with interest-serving, even pandering, messages.

In LCP silence is an opportunity. Earlier in my professorial experience with discussion pedagogy, I internalized classroom silence as failure—thus the sweat running down my spine. I assumed that silence is a failure to be avoided, a sign of incompetence, a waste of time etc. Too slowly I reinterpreted silence as akin to a fruitful reading style, as in *"lectio divina,"* or meditative reading of Holy Scriptures or evocative poetry. Thus I journeyed to an awareness of a type of *"locutio divina,"* or meditative speaking, in healing sessions, or any open type of learning session. A quasi formula comes to mind: In pregnantly critical kairotic moments, less professor talk raises chances of more student voices and reflections, and thus of more learning. Rather than a sign of pedagogical failure, silence in class becomes a valued opportunity made possible by the Learning Community framework.

The modernist Bauhaus dictum finds a new application: Less is more; less professorial talk is more student discussion. Note, however, to amend a teaching citation, not as a professorial "teaching award" but as a student learning award, less professorial speaking may not be more teaching but, hopefully, more learning. The students do the work. LCP is a student-driven experience. Less professor talk provides time and space for student empowerment: If not I, then Who? Well, why not You?

Jose Ortega y Gasset, as I remember his writings on teaching, came to a firm professorial picture. The teacher's vocation is to work toward fashioning a context in which the student becomes able to learn for him or her self. In terms of LCP, this understanding translates into personal and interactional self-and-other understandings, scenes, and situations, in which a group culture of learning is the mission and reward, for each according to his or her style and imperatives.

One operationalization of this task comes through the writings of the psychologist Carl Rogers, who steadfastly refused to answer clients' questions. He insisted, as sedimented in my memory, that clients decide which questions really matter to them; if the answer was worth seeking; whether to research or answer the questions for themselves; and whether to present their findings to the group.

Of course, not all students found this Rogerian move worth the psychological, intellectual, or even financial costs. Indeed, LC members are challenged to answer the ready criticism of those responsible for supporting the teaching/learning institutional moment: We are not paying to have sophomores or seniors trying to educate each other. The professor should earn his or her pay and "teach." We are brought back to alternative models of education in this critique that help sharpen just what LCP is not about as well as what we think it is about.

One outcome LCP is about is what goes under the loose label of a "liberal education." As mentioned earlier, liberal education may mean many things: opposed to the professions; contradictory to brainwashing and indoctrination and catechism; more than training and apprenticeship; less than ideological certitude; etc. (fill in your favorite counter liberal-education idea). Partial answers come from the challenges such as the following: Liberal education assumes a form of liberation, but liberation from what and to what? OK, liberation from ignorance to knowledge. But which form of ignorance and what kind of knowledge? No time here to unpack this problematic, but LCP, at the minimum, assumes that the call is to liberate oneself from conventional certitudinous *aprioris* and unquestioned modes of claiming; to know how to move into an emergent preferred future. More to the issue, each learner comes to liberate self from the core cultural imperatives that were taken for granted. No more cultural chump or identity idiot, who puts personally assimilated cultural versions of how the world really is and should be in place of how the world is descriptively working and how a preferable world appears in the minds' eyes of others with whom we need to fashion that world. We see the world through our culture as though through translucent lenses, without "seeing" how culture predefines that world. Liberal education leads to secular ecstasy: an "ek-static" standing outside the enculturated world, in a possible world in which we all may see more clearly and stand closer together.

So we come to another element in LCP: the call of a distinctly commercial nuance to knowledge, namely, practicalism, pragmatism, instrumentalism, or pragmaticism—as these ripples of transforming knowledge, from *apriori* or formal certitudes into developmental, experimental, experiential, reconstructive, meliorist, and communal tensions, have informed a creative moment in our cultural historical experiment, and one this shrinking globe needs revivified. This pragmatic nuance reemphasizes that intellect is a social and universally shared potential for seeing personal troubles as social issues and, in so doing, working toward a more realistically grounded, inclusive, sustainable, and fair social order.

Education, in this sense, is social in context, content, and modality. Pragmatism suggests that to be educated is to participate in social reconstruction, not only or even possibly in individual acquisition of knowledge. Knowledge, to be efficacious, must be socially intelligent, that is, lead to collective action that addresses critical issues that face us here and now. LCP includes learning skills and values such that only those ideas are real that will be realized by the community facing shared and compelling issues. Knowledge that remains individual slides into that paradox of language that is idiosyncratically individual, that is, akin to a private language—which is a contradiction, since language as means of communication must be intelligible to others with whom we intend to communicate as well as to oneself. So, too, intelligent knowledge is a means to live together with others by solving social issues that are also personal necessities; it involves sharing inclusive identities even as "I" or "We" assert our differentiating identities that must not deny the good and right of other identities to exist. Current instances of international sacred terrorism raise this identity issue into full view. So, also, the collective and personal need for breathable air, potable water, edible food, and sustainable energy points efficacious knowledge to address needed common resources.

A final perspective to fit into the grounding of LCP falls under the broad label of postmodernism, used here in a loose sense to indicate a way of exercising intelligence, and thus becoming educated in today's world, at least the world of liberal education. Elements of postmodernism enter into students' learning in the little LCs of their daily lives. They are firmly aware that they live in a pluralist world; many even believe the university is a heterogeneous community compared with their home bases. Indeed, they typically use the language of "niceness" and "opinion"—two qualities and categories that LCP seeks to go beyond. Be nice to persons, not to analytic objects or intellectual challenges. And no member of the LC is allowed to use the category "opinion" to adjudicate a difference in judgment or decide the characteristics of an analytic object. Differences of opinion need not be joined; after all, they are only opinions. So postmodern students often evade intellect by relegating ideas, judgments, and values to the dustbin of opinion. "Well, that's just my, your, the professor's opinion"—end of discussion and critical engagement. Opinion talk is a vulgar version of postmodern critique and reduction of objective issues to subjective tastes, which, like all tastes, cannot be analyzed, argued, or gone beyond. Matters of mere taste are beyond dispute and remain irresolvable. By analogy with tastes, as in *"de gustibus,"* we may be allowed to suggest that cultural postmoderns work with the dicta *"de opinionibus"* and *"non est disputandum"*: There is no disputing opinions.

Opinion talk affirms a key notion in a postmodern time of "virtual knowledge": The absence of certitudes and nonquestionable foundations for whatever I wish to believe and affirm as known about self, other, and the world. Pedagogically, such postmodern virtual assumptions, typically unexamined by the "true believer," makes bare the aphatic, unsayable nature of meaningful intelligence, or what we may refer to as "wisdom." Contrast this relegation of postmodern and virtual openness in wisdom, values, or understanding of the human condition with the methods, findings, and causal modeling of natural/physical sciences. The latter, no matter how profoundly critiqued theoretically and challenged empirically, lead to technological construction and interventions that, indeed, have real consequences, whether intended or welcomed, desirable or not. Think only of nuclear knowledge and its offspring; genetic interventions and their real and literal offspring; and cyber virtual beings and their apparent offspring, if only in pixels, networks, bots, and clouds that someday may gather and offer access to all accumulated human common sense, knowledge, and aphorisms for living.

Meditation XIX: Why Do Learning Communities Gather at the Circle?

So why do we locomote and come together bodily into a classroom as a circular gathering? What are we to do when we gather? In an age of cyber Web togetherness, what does an LC gain pedagogically by having individual students locomote and share their bodily presences?

What pedagogically relevant differences are there between cyber presence, distance learning, visual courses via TV or disk, educational chat rooms, informative instant messaging, streaming "live" computer/pad visuals, or interactive computer programs? What, if any, pedagogical gain is there in mutual bodily presence that forms a seated circle?

Locomoting allows the fullest and most immediate range of interactional appearances and communicational channels. The physical presence includes full bodily presence in face-to-face encounter; full range of instant emotional presence; simultaneous body languages; real time monitoring of one's and others' appearances and manner; complete cognitive simultaneity; and mutual interactive emergence. "Cyber presence" via electronically channeled mutual presence limits one or another aspect of the full presence of one person to another and of all together. Typing or keying or even mental sequencing, for example, are serial, often delayed, spaced apart, and more or less abstract. Pixelated sequences are actions and, at best, parsed actions, not simultaneously ongoing interactions based on full mutual presence.

Put elliptically, in physical presence "you cannot not appear one to another;" by contrast, in cyber presence "you cannot appear one to another." Appearing one to another is a human universal, one with the dual possibilities of attack or intimacy, but also of learning in a community that loves both learning and one another as learners. And a powerful universal comes along with mutual presence: emotional, facial, and pastime communication and all the pride, shame, delight, and fear that emotional presence makes possible. Full emotional learning is a key possibility within mutual presence. Emotional learning is a primitive, motivational, and universal dimension of fully human learning. Emotional experiences carry the possibilities of love and hate, ease and tension, at their most immediate intensities. LCP attends to, albeit indirectly, safe emotional space/time for students to acquire self-understanding and other- understanding in a preconceptual sense of felt-ideas and known-feelings, not wishful thinking but thinkful wishing. And the key is that emotional knowledge and experience is a primitive universal, more so than the inevitably analytically distinct, potentially exclusivist, and reductionistically self justifying dynamic of mediated cognition of self and of group identification. Emotional self and group identification is immediately felt in mutual presence, and, if apparent, communicated to all present. In others' feelings I experience the universality of my own emotions. Classical authors looked to universal emotions as the grounding for species being, such as love, hope, sympathy, pity, pride, shame, sorrow, and joy.

Once known as felt experience, learners also recognize that others, like myself, need to work through emotions in order to go on living, acting, thinking, and communicating. Emotions generate an inclusivist consciousness of kind among humans, if they are not *apriori* divided by cognitive certitudes and material differences. Such inclusivity is not a certainty, merely a possibility that other dimensions of mutual presence do not offer. Emotions offer the raw material for inclusivity—thus a possible surge in species being from physical and emotional copresence.

Of course, even though the experience of emotions may be pre- or metacognitive and thus bring a potential inclusiveness, specific emotions may lead one to kill another and groups to seek genocide against other groups. Indeed, cognitively guided emotions can kill. Hatred not only motivates killing but justifies it as well. And that is part of the learning that LCP includes. Hatred, for example, is a cognitively informed abstraction from the full humanity the other shares with me. Hatred concentrates only on that aspect of others as less human than I am, so that I may, nay must, kill them. On a lesser frequency, all forms of discrimination and bias follow analogous logic or affective links: a focus on aspects of other we deem hateful; equating the entire self of the other with those selected aspects; abstracting those aspects into essential components of who the other is; identifying those essentialist aspects with metaphors, such as rats, monkeys, or pigs, which are not human, and thus dehumanizing the others; and justifying the elimination of such subhuman life forms as a universal human good. We hate and kill the hated other not as fully present other-as-embodied-self, but, rather, as fully absent other-as-symbolic-member of a subhuman group.

There is no guarantee that LCP will certainly empower participants to overcome such hatred, especially traditionally legitimated and historically reenacted group hatreds. There is, however, at least a possibility that reasonably easeful interaction of mutually present persons may break out of eliminative cognitive entrapments and into affective inclusiveness, if they can accept a culture of love of learning and of one another in the expanded sense within a Learning Community.

Meditation XX: Authenticity and Presence in a Learning Community

Authenticity refers to the way and to the experience through which each participant, the professor and the students, are present to self and to each other. Presence is a strong term. It refers to body, intellect, will, and affective aspects of people who are in each other's communicative field. The mental awareness of each is focused on the situation of the class; its material; the presence of others; and the time they are sharing together. Presence also refers to the overlap of each participant's goals and preparation and willingness to be present here and now. Each is totally here for both self and other. Thus, a sense of existential participation in the group emerges; a sense of belonging that does not threaten one's sense of self but enlarges that sense. In a word, through such presence, one feels, knows, and participates in an empirical moment of self-transcendence.

Both learners and teachers need to be "present" to the learning situation and to each other. We reference this call to be present through such refrains as: "Focus, center, be present here and now. There is no place I would rather be. If there were, I would be there and not here. I come willingly and stay hopefully. Presence undergirds authenticity. The teacher professes presence, his or her own wanting to be here and now." There is no faking authentic presence. I believe that students pick up on presence from the thickly real cues that professors give off as soon as they enter the classroom. The professor can try to fake, to act the part, and even try to deep-act the part by generating the bodily, vocal, announced, and affective cues of authentic presence, but that is likely either to fail in the situation here and now, as students see through the disparity between displayed and actual presence, or to fail in the long run, as professors burn out from the added demands and lost energy of trying to dramaturgically manufacture authentic presence. The first rule, then, is to be existentially and authentically present.

A corollary of the "be authentically present" rule is that the learning of relevance requires that professors discover the teaching/learning modes and outcomes for which they can be authentically present. Learners have different styles of learning; teachers have different styles of teaching. Professors must be able to affirm what they profess in the presence by which they themselves are authentic and can say truthfully, "There is no place I would rather be." Until this mutual and shared affirmation of authentic presence is entered into as a grounding contract of the learning/teaching interaction, the most human of experiences remains, to that extent, alienated, feigned, and forced.

The quest of professor and student to discover themselves as present to one another generates an informing principle of the Learning Community: freedom. Both professor and student discover how they learn and teach from the freedom to explore, experiment, and discuss these explorations and experimentations mutually, as they move on the shared journey of pursuing truth and value. There is no *apriori* or structural answer to the experience and realization of freedom in the classroom. A Socratic perspective posits that freedom to learn demands freedom in learning for both professor and student. In the classroom interaction, then, the meaning of what transpires is an emergent. Learning happens.

The freedom generating emergent learning counters the often *apriori* structural feature of a traditional teacher myth: control. The teacher is supposed to be in control of the classroom. Freedom paradoxically dictates that the teacher is not in control of the classroom in any *apriori* structured sense. Emergent meaning says that the professor never knows what will happen in the classroom, much less what any student or the professor may learn in the interaction. One student referred to the Learning Community as having a sense of "adventure." She caught on to one of the outcomes of LCP: emergence, surprise, adventure, perhaps at magical moments; a sense of psychological flow when the interaction absorbs one's presence. The professor is not likely to experience such a lost sense of individual presence, since the process itself is part of his or her pedagogical presence to the interaction.

Participants' presence announces a temporal orientation that, if authentic, includes all others in shared time. It is a temporal orientation that affirms each person's past, to the extent it is relevant to the present; empowers each one's present as a member of this group, aka, Learning Community; and engages each in the overlapping aspects of each participant's future, and in the shared aspects of those multiple futures. One specification of shared futures, then, is to approach, discern, articulate, and affirm this future *qua* shared, valued, and worthy of calling forth our own commitments, that is, by creating a socially realized imagined future.

Authenticity elicits a sense of shared time together woven out of the particular times that inform the individual lives of participants in the Learning Community. Further, authenticity affirms by and for self, via both self and other, the personal experiences that each brings to the Learning Community. Personal authenticity is realized within a sense of belonging to a social reality greater than the individual, even if realized in the small, temporary, and delimited group of this particular Learning Community. The socially real tension of authenticity follows from an adequate understanding of the tension of a social self—to affirm personal experience and group belonging in the same project for the reconstruction of each.

Historicity is central to our understanding of authenticity. One's personal situation is placed within a shared descriptive and theoretical depiction of each self's historical context. Thus, one specific task of the professor is to contextualize students' personal experiences and quests, within the human struggle writ large, to see, understand, and react to the perennial issues of being human. The texts provide the first depiction of the context; the longer and wider experiences of the professor provides another; the shorter and more distributed experiences of the students provide their existential situation, which is ennobled, empowered, universalized, and affirmed by these shared contexts, even as their experiences are moved excitedly, painfully, or satisfyingly from the received conventional tribal contexts of their primary socializers—as happens to all of us. Thus, the recontextualization of experience renders that experience more authentic by contextualizing it within biographies and, ultimately, a species history.

This process realizes one version of a liberal education. From what are students liberated? From received certitudes about how the world really works! We break out of our received vulgar Platonism that the forms and narratives of my world are those of the species world. Once so universalized, however, the universal stuff of authenticity is reconstructed within the pressing issues of our times, issues that are versions of the universal questions faced earlier, namely, Who am I? What am I to do? Who am I to love? How do I become worthy of being an ancestor? How do I live on the Earth?

What are the key issues of our time, issues that ground both personal and shared authenticity? In the general level of undergraduate courses, I work toward the pedagogical aim of developing, experiencing, and performing "eloquence expressing critical intelligence in pursuit of universal human values." In upper division courses, I am gifted to profess on the great issues facing this generation that have terminal or endtime aspects. The two issues are social tradition and environment: Who am I? Who are you? and How am I and We to live on the Earth?

Authenticity today necessarily means to engage these issues, among others, and to participate in the struggles around their reconstruction and our self-reconstruction. On the positive side, we struggle for identity inclusivity and environmental sustainability for ourselves and others. On the negative side, we struggle against identity exclusivity, such as enemy-making, and against life-system threatening military, economic, religious, and political degradation and pollution of our physical environments. Authenticity is a historically- and situationally-grounded imperative on selves and societies to respond to the temper of our times.

Meditation XXI: Learning Communities are Naturally Intellectual

My best Jesuit professors, refracted here through a many-filtered experience and via synaptic pathways, taught that intellectual work is as natural, fulfilling, and pleasurable, in a classic sense of appetitive goods, as any other natural activity, such as eating, drinking, exercising, praying, or whatever. A human is an *animal intellectuale*, to avoid the reduced sense of the cognates of *rationale* in today's constricted understanding of rationality.

Rationality, for present purposes, refers to a limited, culturally defined, or instrumentally- ordered focus of the more universal and species-defining capability of intelligence. As a species characteristic, intelligence is linked to macrospecies survival, possibilities of cooperative group activities, and to personal action and fulfillment. Intelligence is totally natural and metarational. As such, it is intrinsically pleasing, fulfilling, challenging, and engenders flow experiences, in which self is transcended in engagement with a paradoxically self-absorbing and self-other fulfilling action orientation. The naturalness of intelligence comes in the narrative and language that is native to each of us as participants in shared communities, public goods, and group dynamics.

This understanding of intelligence as naturally pleasing and fulfilling counters the oft enshrined dictum that "knowledge maketh a bloody entry." True, many kinds of knowing require extensive effort, and one may experience the effort as strenuous, demanding, and, at times, frustrating, as I surely have. Assimilation is sometimes difficult; vocabularies are memory-driven to a degree; subjunctives in Spanish, prepositions in English, and verb forms in German are too often mysterious and frustrating to nonnatives. The bloodiness of the learning, then, comes from personal frustration with an imagined or imposed standard and timetable, for learning ten new words, for example, or the future-perfect tense.

LC Pedagogy remains totally committed to the inherent natural attractiveness of learning generated by wonder, challenge, living together, and issue-resolving. So, too, is any sporting, gaming, climbing, risk-taking activity. LC Pedagogy suggests that the bloodiness of the entry comes not from the act of learning but from the extrinsic scoring of that act, or comparing it to others, or needing it for practical immediate goals—all empirical likelihoods extrinsically attached to our learning but not intrinsic to the act of intelligence itself.

Meditation XXII: Classical Foundation Stones of Learning Community Pedagogy

Coming out of the Judeo-Christian tradition, LC Pedagogy understands the material world as somehow the primary creative appearance of Divinity. The material world is the first text, as it were, of Divine revelation, a text prior to and never exhausted by the socially mediated textual sources of sacred canons. The Bible, for example, may have no mention of viruses, tsetse flies, and bacteria, but creation includes them, and so too does the challenge to name, rename, and ultimately deny names to Divinity. The relation of sacred canon to material creation emerges as one of the oldest yet currently-relevant questions, as human intelligence is drawn to learn how to respond ever more adequately to its material surroundings. As part of a transcendent religious world, then, LC Pedagogy understands all humans as creatures in the image and likeness of Divinity. All humans! In their image God created them as the inclusivist, not the sexist, tradition in "Genesis" would have it.

The claim is sometimes made that all Western thought is a series of footnotes to Plato; and Plato learned from Socrates, as his teacher. Again, what relevance to LC Pedagogy is Socrates' well-known claim about himself after quizzing reigning types of Athenians, such as politicians, poets, and artisans, and after trying to make sense of the Delphic Oracle's labeling him the wisest of Athenians? What was his claim to wisdom? Only this: that those he quizzed thought they knew what they did not know about the really important issues of human existence, whereas he, Socrates, knew that he did not know. Only in his awareness of his ignorance was he wiser than those who thought they knew.

Concomitant with the birth of Western rationality is a condemnation of certitude, *apriorisms*, and unreflective "but of course" understandings of the world and human existence. Only in this is a human worthy of wisdom: The person knows that knowledge of the important issues of being is a continuous public and shared quest for wisdom in the service of the greatest aspirations of our species—the true, the good, and the beautiful—which may, in contemplation, be one, even if it never comes to be in action. From the truth of wisdom as a continual quest comes the personal corollary: An unexamined life is not worth living. Such examination is not the peevish navel gazing of pop stressmakers, but the hardeyed and ennobling quest for shared wisdom to build a polis, a community, of freedom and equity—goals far beyond the reach of Athenian slaves, and still beyond the reach of many in global megalopolies laced with slums and sprinkled with the homeless.

The absence of certitude makes room for the rise of wonder. Another classical inheritance is Aristotle's assertion that all knowing begins with wonder—a thaumaturgic experience that ranges from surprise to amazement. The experience of wonder awakens and motivates the person to engage in a search for learning. Wonder-filled learning is an intrinsic self-motivating experience. It need not be driven from the outside with whips or carrots or grades. LC Pedagogy, then, arises from instances that hopefully elicit wonder in learners. To the extent that professors are able to elicit wonder, to that degree students are likely to be self-motivated. This wonder-filled learning, in turn, requires freedom amidst discipline, since wonder is both individual referenced and species relevant. Think of the actional truths experienced in puzzles, games, riddles, problems, antinomies, hatred, love—wonder-filled experiences, each in its own way. The housekeeping window at the beginning of each class is one possible source of wonder at the current events that inform our lives today, regardless of our different ages and statuses.

Pedagogy itself is a wonder-filled process. And since wondering is a natural response to the strange or challenging or problematic, the learning motivated by wonder is natural as well. So learning is as natural as any bodily function and as pleasurable in its own domain. Second, as natural and pleasurable, learning is just as intrinsically motivating as it is intrinsically motivated. Analogous to the old definition of a living being as that which moves itself by itself, a human being is that which learns itself by itself. In the domain of humanistic learning at least, too much of formal, institutionalized learning may violate the previous experiences of learning, as species natural and personally motivating.

The classical Greek ideals reflect a *paideia* pedagogy. *Paideia* suggests that youth learn to learn and to act virtuously through socialization into a noble and worthy community. Learning has a public source and outcome. Learning is political in the generic sense of making one competent and worthy for life in the polis, the community. Outside the community, one would be reduced to a private person, an "*idiote*," i.e., an idiot, a totally particularistic and mute animal. Outside of society, a human would be an angel or a beast. For good or ill, we are adequately human only within communities; so pick your community well and struggle for the right of all to pick communities of intellect, justice, peace, and beyond.

Then another historical move comes within Christian culture as Augustine learns, because God is his teacher; and teaching-learning becomes an earthly exercise in the enlightening wisdom and creative love of Divinity reenacted within human bodies and among human persons struggling to fashion the City of God on earth. Augustine adumbrates utopian thinking, a component of LC Pedagogy. What would you say a well-ordered society or well-formed person looks like?

Take a step with the Angelic Doctor himself, Thomas Aquinas. This Angelic Doctor and major source of scholastic thinking is said to have made assertions that reenforce pedagogy as process and not as formulae or repetition. Exiting his cell after meditation, he is reported to have said, "All I have written is straw"—and straw, even in today's world of few stables, is recognizable as a euphemism for that which horses deposit on straw. If Aquinas relativized the contribution of his writings, we know that certitude and essence are temporary transitions in the process of learning.

Even in his theology, Aquinas knew that if we know God as "that," we simultaneously know God as "not that." No name or category exhausts or captures the meaning of God. As a Jesuit professor professed in my hearing, God is "transobjective." So central to learning what we may take as salvific, we travel along the "*via negativa*": Whatever we assert about God and salvation we must, simultaneously, negate. So, too, with the perennial questions about what it means to be human, even here and now.

Meditation XXIII: How to Spend Learning Time When Community Gathers

LCP, in principle, may occur within any mode of mutual presence, from face-to-face to pixel-to-pixel, from bodily presence to cyber-streaming. Given the trajectory toward distance learning and the emphasis on technological extensions of the teaching-learning act, what does mutual bodily presence offer that justifies the costs and commitments of locomotion?

Students' obligations are reading, participation, taking exams (written or oral), and papers. The course is "student driven." Its motor is students as learners becoming self- and other-aware, if they are not already, of what they profess as participants in the universal necessity of living intellectually, and loving one another in this living and learning together.

For a while, I started out class with "any questions?" Virtually no one asked a question, except for occasional format, exam, paper, or task-oriented questions. I think I remember but a single substantive question. Most questions concerned grade-related issues such as exams, participation, and attendance. It was clear that students expected that I was to perform and they would passively observe without expressing eagerness or engagement. This response was typical in thirty-to-forty-student social-psychology classes. I inferred that for a student to ask a substantive question about the subject matter or readings implied that this student cared; that he wanted to read; that she would be willing to take a risk of admitting she did not understand something, and thought it important that she try; or that he was willing to cooperate with the professor, and thus risk aligning with his "team" vs. the team made up of students manifesting aloof concern, if not indifference.

Over time, LC Pedagogy evolved and pointed to the first moments of the class gathering, whether reading was done or not. That is, I tried to situate students to experience "wonder," the inviting experience of an affectively suffused cognitive learning. The light that came on was the necessary function of positive affect, of a pleasing emotional engagement with the learning process.

The transitional learning of subject matter and area of student competence and interest eventually generated the idea of "housekeeping," a term and process I adopted from the experience of my wife, a long time successful professor who knew how to engage students' lives into the pedagogical process. Housekeeping elicits the liminal subject matter emerging from students' experiences of current events, and it provides a space/time for realizing LCP as a process that encompasses the three "texts": reading materials, the primary analogue of a text; the existential "texts" of students' biographical experiences; and the "texts" of current emerging events, interpreted in the classroom discussions. In a word, housekeeping enables students to experience links to the world, to their biographies, and to the assigned texts as subject matter for both shared learning and realizing a learning experience through an emerging classroom discussion, without walls but within lives and contexts.

Housekeeping empowers students to choose a subject or question relevant to their lives; it implies the relevance of LC subject matter to events that make up their lives; it is a low-risk venture, especially after a few exemplars and supportive responses by professor and students; and it blurs the line between the professor's team and students' team. On the other side, more traditional students sometimes feel and think that housekeeping is a waste of time. As one student remarked, with an obvious edge of anxious frustration and unrequited disbelief, "We spent half the class on housekeeping and it's still continuing!"

Once housekeeping is over, student "catalysts" are responsible for energizing the discussion, for helping us "seminarate"—itself a somewhat risky neologism, but intended to do what neologisms help us to do, i.e., focus on the newness or at least nontraditionalness of what we as members of an LC think we are about. In brief, during the time we spend in each other's bodily presence, four sources of subject matter are at hand: in common we have the assigned readings, the shared housekeeping experience, the emergent group discussions about any of these, and the didactic presentations by the professor as short commentaries, more visual presentations, or as handouts—often short pieces from current newspapers or cartoons relevant to issues arising from current readings or topics. Interlacing these sources are the comments from the personal experiences of students, hopefully, and professors. LCP creates space/time for different learning styles and exercising different modes of relating to materials and each other through reading, writing, presenting, introducing current events or experiences by creating "objects" placed inside the class circle, leading discussions, and participating in discussions.

Meditation XXIV: Personalized Learning Community Reflections on Professor, Student, And Higher Education System

As a "professor," the central legitimation of one's presence is the intrinsic good of the clients, as the professor as well as the clients learn to judge what is good here and now. Reflecting on formal education in the USA, I see a double wrong in the "delivery system," shall we say, of the university, in relation to the good of the student. Consider the story of the suicide of an MIT student as an exemplar of the issue of the university and the good of the student.

The student suicide came amidst earlier national survey data that indicated reported stress at an all time high among high school graduates entering college (*New York Times* Magazine, April 28, 2002; *The Chronicle of Higher Education Special Report*: "Today's Anguished Students," September 4, 2015, pp. A38ff.). In general, it appears that student stress goes up and a sense of psycho-social wellbeing goes down during college years. LC Pedagogy builds on an interpretation of the rhetoric and issue-definition of incoming students as moving along with this systemic trend. On the one hand, each entering first year class is reported as more accomplished than the last, according to usual indicators of rankings and standardized test scores. On the other hand, constant attention is given to "grade inflation." Note the transition from accomplishments and preparation to objectified measurements: grades. In part, the solution implied is to turn grade distribution into a war of all against all, with increased competition and a restriction of top grades or other indicators of learning success. Grades are objectively measured. As are rarely given; and the grade distribution is fit to a "normal curve."

I consider this model as misguided. In a few words, student performances can be arrayed and ranked to an extent. As Warren Buffett is reported to have said: You can recognize the 00s and the 100s but the middle is rather indiscernible. And as I was taught in measurement classes in sociology and economics, there is no zero point from which to begin cardinal measurement. Second, even if performance is translated into numbers that reflect merely ordinal and not absolute measurement, there is no objective way to peg those numbers into a letter system: What number is an A and what is an A-, B, or C? If you have never tried this, you have missed a moment of godlike creation of letter grades out of no letters—an analogy of *"creatio ex nihilo sui et subjecti"* ("a creation out of no relevant subjects"). And, of course, once a professor has arbitrarily made a sequence of numbers into an empirically unrelated sequence of letters, the letters are translated back into numbers, even to the third or more decimal point. This is translation become transmogrification. And students, who are rational actors for the most part, know and play the game well, that is, how they generated the scores that got them into top- ranked universities in the first place. Finally, the retranslated numbers become a Grade Point Average that is then used by postcollege bidders in the human capital market to judge the quality of the products, aka graduates.

As a professional, however, I believe, but do not have the courage to defend my beliefs with my livelihood, that grades exist in a fiduciary and confidential moral space shared by the student and the professor, much as medical records, religious confessions, counseling judgments, and legal communications are, or were, bound by professional confidentiality to protect the privacy-good of the client, patient, sinner, or mentally challenged person. We are beginning to know about increasing invasions of privacy and the takeover of clients' goods by bureaucratized institutions, typically for profit or power, which is not in itself the good of the client. So I believe that grades should remain confidential between the student and the professor, and the university should merely store them.

I do not believe that grades should be systematically made available to third parties such as employers and postgraduation institutions for students. If institutions wish to make hiring or entrance decisions about students, then let them do their own testing and not coopt and violate professors' and students' shared evaluative communication about the students' learning. Such objectification, transmogrification, and cooptation of a professor's summary of students' learning corrodes and, in turn, transforms the learning interaction. It transfoms student learning from a goal to a means, from intrinsically valuable and inherently good to extrinsically useful and probabilistically expedient.

Students and professors now know and operate within a system that judges courses by the grades they generate, which, in turn, constitute probabilities that a student may gain entry into particular occupations or training niches. Thus, grades are commodified for the next market evaluation, and the professor-student relationship is commodified and market-rationalized as well. Indeed, an earlier Carnegie study found that the split and tension between learning or education and grading or training pervades higher education at all levels: administration, professors, and students.

Why, then, go to college? To get a job; to get an education; to compete in the occupational marketplace; to become a more humane person; to be more inclusive and sustaining and ennobling. These goals are now set off against each other, though they need not be. Take "privatization," revenue stream, or grants as indicators of quality, placements as markers of teaching, or whatever outcome you prefer as indicative of the quality the educational institution provides, and translate it back into a confidential fiduciary-interactional outcome between professor and student.

This short excursus brings us back to the heart and soul of a student-professor relationship. "Grade tension" is, I believe, a dynamic factor in the stress, abulia, and other psycho-social contingencies of students; the educational delivery system has socialized them not to learn but to perform that grade-producing act that defines education at the highest levels of societal and governmental self-understanding: "Study for the test." Learning is replaced by testing and teaching becomes training to take tests. And as any educator knows, tests are reductionist and outcomes are commodified. I would be stressed too, would not you, *verdad*?

Again, by analogy with other professional domains, just as the health delivery system paradoxically sometimes generates higher probabilities of illness in the very process of trying to heal (i.e., iatrogenic illness)—as when you go to the hospital for a hip replacement and come out with a titanium hip and an infection—so, too, I suggest we look at the delivery system of higher education for signs of "pedagogenic mental illness," such as stress, depression, and psycho-social dis-ease as unintended byproducts of the production of grades as the means to assortative market positioning of graduates.

Professors and students live in this somewhat contradictory tension of institutionalized learning. If I may be allowed a recollection, this institutionalized tension was vividly made known to me when I was in the Jesuit Novitiate during an assignment in another community, with another responsible authority other than the usual Novitiate administration. At an after-dinner review of our performance, the "spiritual father" noted that he was held to a twofold task toward our youthful development as possible members of the Jesuit community. He was to fulfill two functions toward us, namely, "*formare ac probare*," which I took to mean "educate us into Jesuit life and simultaneously evaluate our progress toward that life." Just so does a professor face her or his students: to open the way to an educated life and to evaluate their movement toward that mode of being human. Nowhere does it say grade them in a statistically determined distribution, rank those distributions, put a scarcity restriction on those rankings, disseminate those rankings directly or indirectly to third parties, and make present status and future rewards dependent on those rankings. Institutionalized learning and the vital good of students are corrupted in pursuit of some of its intrinsic goals by the ways in which institutionalized grading is constructed, made public, and marketed.

Students, for the most part, appear to have internalized this commodified rendition of experiencing, communicating, and "measuring" what they have learned. As a commodity, grades are kept scarce: Fewer As are supplied than are demanded. Thus a market emerges for high-priced grades, and students compete against each other not to learn, *per se*, but to win the measures of what they, institutionally speaking, are supposed to have learned. These commodities are not consumed. They become investment capital, goods that students interpret as down payments on their futures: professional schools, graduate schools, careers, financial security, and an attractive—in every sense—spouse; and thus they are supposed to have the fulfilled life that a university that defines its distinguishing characteristic as "Catholic" preaches, along with idealized versions of Catholic charity, with a dose of justice for those who chart their way through institutionalized paths of the university.

LCP tries to mitigate and restrain the commodification of grades by distributing them within the comfort range and past achievement intervals of the students. Eliminating grade anxiety allows for more soul-searching and critical, deep learning to occur. It creates some space/time for students to experience themselves as autonomous learners and enjoy the feeling of cognitive and affecttive fulfillment in a learning outcome experienced as a purely human good.

LCP has no final answer to the commodification of learning through marketable grades. A suggestion that some courses be "ungraded," such as required "wisdom learning," renders the proposed solution susceptible to mockery, as "lacking standards" in the context of the university's looking outside for others' measures of the university's success, instead of operationalizing its own "genius" to create a newly-autonomously moral citizen.

Meditation XXV: Premise, Goals, Means, Principle Informing Learning Community

Given the format of the pedagogy, what are the premise, goals, means, and principles informing it?

Premise: Professor needs to project an embodied trust that students can believe and realize, even if they are not quite sure what trust is, how it arises, or how it is known for sure. Trust is always promissory. The professor projects a nonjudgmental persona and the emergent miniculture of the LC is that no students are judged, "graded," coerced, or punished for any intellectual effort, intervention, or initiative.

One operationalization of nonjudgmental trust is to work at separating ego from issue. Issues become objects that rest in the center of the circle. Issues-as-objects are present for everyone's evaluation, criticism, or reconstruction. Within the bounds of LC discourse, objects are treated as such—as objects to be fashioned and refashioned. Not so with egos: They remain off base from object-treatment. Egos are persons. Persons are sacred and not to be remade from the outside by others. Issues-as-objects are fair game for any response within the reasonable and civil culture of the LC.

Of course it is difficult for the speaker, as well as the hearer, to separate ego from issue; the professor fails at this repeatedly in the same mode as more youthful students, but hopefully by now with less animus. What self says comes out as an object with self's stamp of origin on it. To attack the said object is symbolically, if indirectly, to attack the self who spoke the object. And selves are quick to defend their spoken objects with an affect and intensity that belies the object but bespeaks the self. Separating ego from issue is a lifelong challenge and essential to LC dynamics. It lays the groundwork for each participant to recognize the other as person, even as object to queried, and, in turn, be empowered to expect such recognition when the shoe is on the other foot.

The separation of ego from issue makes space for student self-empowerment as emerging intellectuals. To the degree that they make that separation, they gradually learn to analyze objects without attacking persons; and, reciprocally, the interactional exchanges in that safe, self- space offer opportunities for each student self to speak what self is thinking, feeling, repeating, or fearing without one's self being attacked in turn. Thus, the dialectic of other-recognition and self-empowerment is a tango of mutual trust in selves and objective analysis of objects.

Students, then, experience what interactionist social-psychology finds at the base of healthy selves: worthy competence, values, authenticity, and esteem. These groundings for intellectual selfhood are not the objects measured by grades. The premise of separating ego from issue implies separating self from grades. LC Pedagogy tries to get students out from the artificially competitive point-scoring mentality of institutionalized grades based on constructs of unambiguously right or wrong answers. Such measurement theory is appropriate for certain kinds of learning and training and subject matters, if properly understood. For example, it is absolutely true, we assume, that Columbus thought he discovered a new world—or did he think it was an old world in 1492, so that 1493 is a wrong year? Yet, to assert that Columbus discovered America (or was it China?) in 1492 is a gross quasifactual reduction and, indeed, wrong if the runes of the northeast coastal areas are correct that Nordics were here first, and the later emergence of the name of America came from an Italian cartographer.

Thus so, a professor in an LC works to wean students from tests and test grades. For example, no comments other than a memory-aid label or two are made on the artificial genre and forced performance that is an examination designed to produce outcomes to which others apply letters, numbers, or both, transformed from one to the other, as though there were a metric or translation matrix for such equivalences. The first response a student makes upon the return of a "graded product" is immediately to look at the grade, even on the back pages of papers. Professors wonder if students ever read their marginalia.

The absence of comments on tests, however, bothers some students eager to learn how to do better on the next test. The frustrated reaction of some students to comment-free test results parallels that of students committed to taking notes in class, and, perhaps, unknowingly using the number and organization of notes taken as an indicator of the worth of the class time. A student approached this professor after one give-and-take session and, red in the face, blurted out, as he slapped his open notebook with the back of his free hand, "Look, I haven't taken a single note all class!" Not much the professor could do for that well-trained student. Weaning students from tests frees them from one institutionalized source of zero-sum gaming, forced ranking competition, and alienated understandings of self-as-intellectual, though not from evaluation of critical thinking and expression, which is essential to learning/teaching, in spite of the inevitable limitations of any single evaluator.

Goal: To live competently in a democratic community and strive for a well-ordered, just, sustainable, and peaceful society. That is the "test" toward which LC Pedagogy is aiming and by which it is to be evaluated. It is the "object outcome," in some sense, but not in the sense and structure that grades have acquired in the formal system. By contrast, this is not training for a positivistic institutionalized test. Such "teaching to the test" governs the intellectual life by what the powerful who make the test and enforce it build into it in terms of outcome values and attitudes, in the service of reproducing the dominant culture hierarchy. LC Pedagogy, paradoxically combines communitarian and libertarian themes: to build community and, in so doing, to realize self in a value-based understanding of person as essentially a social self, not an abstracted and autonomous individual.

Means: The structure, processes, and contents of the class format: reading, reflection, group discussion, scope of professional responses and those of peers, reinterpretation of self's understanding, reconstruction of self and "class" as a stand-in for society. As students enter into the dynamics of a dialogical, democratic class, there is beginning hope for persons around the globe to do the same. LC Pedagogy is cosmopolitan democracy writ small.

Principle: Here's the key: The principle of learning is intellect and, thus, learning is intrinsically meaningful and mentally pleasurable. The method is reasoning. The content is empirical in the broadest sense, reflecting what I learned as an "incarnational" view of the world, or what pragmatists may refer to as a life built on an ever reformable scientific knowledge about, and understandings of, the world and our relationships to that world and to each other. The assumptions are nonfoundational, contingent, and reformable. It is a nondisciplinary version of the scientific method writ interactionally democratic. Intelligence is contrasted with interests, ideology, and all forms of imagined exclusivist certitudes. Intelligence deals with futures, which are contingent; futures are shared and emerge from collaborative interactions with that world and each other.

In today's world, these futures are also pluralistic, global, and species-linked. Until today, humans have been ecosystem or regional actors. Now we are biospheric actors. We no longer affect only our regions or neighborhoods but also the entire society, as we travel on our Earth, as well as the Earth itself. Our cognitive dem-ocracy—or "people-governing" dynamic—needs to become a biosphere-ocracy—or "environmental-governing"dynamic.

Interests prefer me over you, us over them. Ideology posits my world in place of yours. Both interests and ideology work toward my or our futures to the exclusion of you and your futures. Intelligence works to see through and beyond interests and ideology. It eschews certitude and, most of all, transcendental posits allowing us to dehumanize all who are not identified as welcome in my transcendental world.

One version of intellectual dialogue free of interests, ideology, and transcendentalism was the ideal of "free-floating intellectuals" (Karl Mannheim's *freischwebende Intelligenz*). Another is the American pragmatic ideal of a future community in which the recurrent issues of persons living together in common are continually readdressed from an expanding moral and inclusivist perspective that motivates meliorative action to fashion a more well-ordered society. This version of pragmatism, I am told, was in part fired by Kant's description of "pragmatic faith" as a bet against the odds for a certain preferred outcome of my present action. Intelligence serves pragmatic faith, a democratic pluralistic rendition of *"fides quaerens intellectum,"* or faith seeing understanding.

The format of Learning Community Pedagogy, therefore, is geared to invite students into this dialogical process and to acquire the pragmatic faith, shared confidence, social trust, and moral commitment to share it with others, especially with those who are most unlike self in a continual species effort to build a well-ordered society that is inclusive and sustainable.

Meditation XXVI: Learning Community Works Best in Safe Space and Time

A student writes that she feared thinking about and questioning her received ideas and sustaining narratives about God and, for her personally, about Jesus. On the other hand, in campfire discussions of such religious issues, she is invited to engage in just that. This is a scary move and one that is paradigmatic for the informative principle of LC Pedagogy, *one must question precisely that which was taken as unquestionable: The certain becomes the contingent* in the never-ending quest for a just and moral life shared with others.

This informative principle lies at the heart of intellect supported by faith. At the same time, it suffuses one's sense of cognitive security and, perhaps, sanity. As a phenomenologist may say, my idealized assumptions generate the world in which I think I live. Yet that world is a cognitive construction built on faith—secular as well as religious, but always on a certain kind of unquestioned faith. A sociologist would add that the taken-for-granted world is constructed out of materials—ideas, images, metaphors, axioms, proverbs, of-course statements—that are the stuff of socio-cultural *"realities"* (I always put that word in italics in my mind's eye), which then become the subject matter of personal worldviews.

LC Pedagogy invites questioning of the unquestioned and making contingent what was certain. The invitation comes in the form of others willing to do the same and to support each others' pilgrimage. The culture of the LC then becomes a culture in which intellect is dually realized, that is, first it is made real both in interaction among participants and within participants, between their received certainties and their emergent shared understandings relevant to the inclusive values all are seeking; and second it is brought to an awareness in participants that they are, indeed, explicitly engaged in and self-consciously agents of this awareness, of this construction. The double meaning of "realization" as making real and becoming aware of what one takes as real mirrors such a breakthrough. And such breakthroughs can be scary, threatening, and rejected as dangerous, erroneous, or even heretical, if read in the received narratives that participants, including myself, bring to the LC.

So I take "intellect" as the primordial domain within which we humans work out the possibilities of our species being. Each of us can fill in what he or she would posit as the universal efficacious and coping possibilities of humans, as both species knowers and actors. I have residual images of intellect as a free-floating form or force enveloping all human society, and in which all humans participate— a sort of Platonic or Avicennaean all-encompassing mind that provides the cognitive space and copresent time in which we have a chance of shared knowing. Later in my education, this universalizable mind was rooted in Thomistic ideas of connatural knowledge, given with ensoulment in all humans, or of enlightened grace sprinkled somewhat mysteriously but generously among all persons. Finally, exposure to American social pragmatism located intellect in collective responses to common issues of shared living, responses derived from cooperative to appropriately antagonistic attempts to fashion a more inclusive future.

In this foundational sense of intellect, reason is a derivative-disciplined formulation of means-ends for achieving a reasonably agreed-upon yet emergent future. In Max Weber's scheme, intellect deals with the interfaces of traditional, affective, and value-oriented aspects of what humans are willing to take as knowledge that realizes the world in which both they and others live. LC

Pedagogy, then, seeks to elicit social intellect in each participant. This invitation works well with the majority of students in LCs, but only in so far as they themselves respond to it.

The limits of LC Pedagogy would be the limits of violated intellects: arational fanaticism, posited fundamentalism, certitudinous ideology, heteronomous cognitive control—as when a believer says that his spiritual/economic/philosophical/military guru-authority does all his thinking for him, a condition we may reference as "brain washing" or, more aptly, intellect-otomy. If there is no intellect, there is no learning, only assimilation, indoctrination, dogmatism. Pedagogy, then, just as a university, is an ongoing conversation (a "turning toward one another") about possibilities of sharing a more inclusive future.

Meditation XXVII: Learning and Values in a Learning Community

Learning in its naturalness is a function of values. Pursuing a more desirable future and fulfilling one's sense of self and identity is a process of learning that has a likelihood of seeming as natural as breathing, indeed of play, challenge, adventure, and games, i.e., it feels natural and sometimes pleasurable. In some of the ancient resonances that bounce around in my thinking, learning fulfills a natural appetite in pursuit of universal values.

An indicator of the valued aspect of one's learning is the presence of emotion, affect, and passion. A person "heats up" when in pursuit of her or his values. The chase is hardly debilitating; rather, it is energizing like a generator: The pursuit recharges one's power sources. In a word, learning in this sense is not the abstracted ideal of scientism or other reductionisms. Learning is not accompanied by neutrality, disconnected objectivity, pure reasoning, or any of the other typifications that were taught to me and that I unreflectively taught for years. There are issues of bias, interpretation, and selectivity embedded in these assertions, but I believe that recognizing the function of passion as an indicator of values more likely makes these issues apparent and negotiable. Denying or repressing both the cognitive function of values and the energizing play of passions only makes them invisible, and turns their impact, commingled with conclusions and uncritical negotiation, into an issue of integrity, honesty, and truthfulness, rather than a known, accepted, and tractable set of ever-present conditions of learning.

Learning, then, is experienced as passion and driven by commitment to potentially universal values. These reflections provide an interactional and experiential foundationalism for learning that sidesteps the blinders of cognitive, ideological, or religiously hegemonic foundationalism and *apriorism*. I come to class with a mix of values and an occasional burst of passion or a slip into ego defense. These two existential aspects of learning are never totally foreseeable and controllable. They are the content of another of our lifelong quests. So my current passionate values were not always such. Two universalizing quests inform my learning from two positive values that generate sufficient passion to keep me getting out of bed, entering the (class)room, and, so far, not burning out.

The two positive substantive values are inclusivist self-understandings of relationships with others, which define inclusivist grounds for each other's identity as a species being, and sustainable understandings of one's relationships with the physical environment as a biospheric interactor. The contextual and grounding value that informs these substantive values is intellect. I am not a philosopher, so in the spirit of these meditations on learning, what I intend by the term "intellect" is a cognitive power, dynamic, and interactional resource that is available to all competent humans by virtue of their species being. What I intend by intellect takes form by contrasting it with reason, ideology, transcendent faiths, authoritative texts, and any hegemonic relationship in which the learner locates the source of his or her learning in something or someone outside of self.

In my own learning, there are three institution-based levels of passion and values and the learning they make possible: intellect and the quest for universal human values, in the campfire of humanities texts; intellect and the beginnings of disciplined inquiry into substantive species values, that is, self and other identities; and the issue of interacting with the environment in sustainable ways.

Meditation XXVIII: Some Learning Community Student Responses

Students comment that LCP has defining characteristics of process and norm. One student felt that class sometimes had an adventurous dynamic. LCP, as student-driven and democratic, does not have preordained, structured dynamics with previewed outcomes. There is an adventurous sense of moving into an unknown. No one, including the professor, knows where the class is heading. This is part of the understanding of an adventure: stepping into something of an unknown trajectory, yet having a sensitized awareness of the good that is sought, a sort of secular Holy Grail quest.

Another student aimed at a similar description, by noting the unusual freedom exercised in the class, beginning with the professor. This follows from positing freedom as an organizational principle of LC and, thus, an informing principle of its pedagogy. Professorial freedom models student freedom, and freedom motivates critical learning. This kind of "freedom for" the pursuit of truth is mirrored in a student's observation that she liked the "freedom from" the pressure to answer a question or make a comment in a "go around the circle and respond to an issue" exercise, which occurs periodically in LCP. "Freedom from" insures that the student may always claim a "pass," as in a card game, and choose not to respond without prejudice or punishment. Such moments are not "graded;" and having moments of participation outside the grading process realizes "freedom for" the students. LCP has grading moments but also tries to experience ungraded moments as well.

How would you parse a minority, female sophomore's struggle to possess her intellect and her faith in the face of *apriori* family-internalized imperatives? Her struggle and pain are reflected in the following statement, paraphrased from her last paper, which was written for the section of a prior core course curriculum titled "God":

How I was raised taught me never to question God's existence, for to question Him would be like committing a sin. This core curriculum section has made me confront questions buried deep inside of myself. I was terrified to speak them, because I feared that I would be destined for Hell. Facing these questions, however, and contemplating the answers to them, has only served to strengthen my faith in God. . . . Now I no longer blindly follow anyone else."

After this introduction, she penned a rather lengthy poem that expressed her newly possessed and self-aware experience of faith.

Consider another minority, female senior student in a 400-level sociology course on society and identity. Her words, paraphrased below, reflect a struggle for a realized identity and identity dynamics that, in spite of stereotypes, biases, and conflicts have a chance of being inclusive, experiential, authentic, and even leading to personal fulfillment. As can be seen, she also discussed the presence and outcomes of stereotypes in society, a reality that is "prior in every way" to the individual.

I discovered a similarity between my final research results into stereotyping and concluding thoughts about society and personal identity at the end of our class. At that time, I also felt somewhat negative about the concept that the individual has less power to shape society than society has to shape the individual. It made me feel "down" to realize this, since I've always felt that I could behave however I wanted, in accordance with my own choices. Now, my only modicum of optimism regarding this issue is, no matter the major influence society has to define what we are and who we become, we are neither determined nor prevented from experiencing joy in our lives.

My ultimate realization about solving the issue of stereotyping was that there is nothing that can be done to solve the problem. We can attempt a multitude of different behaviors to eradicate prejudice and stereotypes, but they will never be fully eliminated. Individuals will continue to categorize and rank others they encounter based on their prior backgrounds and experiences. While this conclusion may sound depressing, I nonetheless feel there is room for consolation; for just as we must accept that although our identities are shaped by society we can still live happy lives, so, too, we must accept that until there are no more controversies and world conflicts, we can be joyful that we live in a world that allows us to meet many different kinds of people, who offer a variety of wonderful things to society. The more we break down the stereotypes we are currently forced to live with, then better people we will become, and the greater will be the understanding we have of the world in which we live.

This student courageously accepted the reality of society as prior to the individual, and weighed the influence this has on both her own identity experience and the ways in which she experiences and bestows identities on others. She responds to her newly possessed descriptions and understandings of self and world with a move toward reconstruction of both self and society—a move toward the virtuous life. She realizes the distinction between efficacious action and moral action. They are not the same, and the former is not a criterion for the morality of action or personal fulfillment. Indeed, we are often called to act morally in the full face of the realization that the action is, in all likelihood, doomed to fail. The good is not coextensive with the efficacious. In the full admission that societal norms and pressures, social prejudgments and stereotyping, scarce resources and inequality, and the resulting grievances and conflicts are beyond any foreseeable solution, she reaffirms the call to live joyously and work continuously to counter these likely nonsolvable human conditions. We must quietly admire such radical realism and positive courage. Our human vocation to live a virtuous life presents a rigorous and endless moral claim on all of us.

Experience with learning communities leads to the observation that many students already know many of the humanistic "truths," issues, principles, dilemmas, and "big ideas" that academic professionals wish to communicate. They know them, however, in other media and narratives than those of classical, intellectual, disciplinary, or received texts. They know them through TV, the Internet, videos, movies, and music. Over and over again, students in their presentations refer to such media, both to recall what they themselves discovered earlier and rediscovered in the LC and to reinterpret what they had once enjoyed or been moved to remember as meaningful.

A key pedagogical move in a Learning Community, then, is to universalize, both historically and spatially, the often individually-interpreted meanings as echoing perennial issues of the human condition or social existence. Thus, contemporary Rock or Rap may echo the Sufi mystic Rumi, of the fourteenth century, or the squabbles of roommates may parallel those of the Forest People, the Pygmies descended from ancestors living for thousands of years in the Ituri rainforests. So students learn to think of themselves as inheriting much of human experience that went before and, yet, struggling with issues that appear to be intrinsic to our species' experience.

LC experience is here and now. Yet it may expand that experience to others who came before, and with societal dynamics that inform all human living together. This realization enlarges the humanity of the students and moves them to form more inclusive understandings of themselves, their values, and how they act toward others and to the natural world.

Meditation XXIX: Innocence versus Seeing in a Learning Community

Learning Community Pedagogy builds on the assumption of the primacy and universality of intellect. As such, intellect often has one outcome that is both ennobling and scary, like the painful satisfaction of so-called "growing pains" in those young enough to be physically developing. Those who profess an LC Pedagogy share a vocation to challenge self's and each other's innocence and certitudes. LC experience uproots the consolation derived from "well, of course" statements and convictions. LC experience may redefine your previous life, and it holds up the promise of expanded meaning in place of innocence.

After passing through the social reinterpreting fire of LCP, students are welcome to repossess, reaffirm, and reassert previous beliefs, assumptions, and values, but now they are realized as self-aware and freely chosen intellectual products, not the unexamined results of genes, divine inspiration, blind subordination, unexamined socialization, and/or obedience to another's authority. LCP does not seek conversion but enlightenment, responsibility, and accountability. The learner's beliefs, even if substantively the same as before LC experience, are qualitatively different. Their grounding is in the responsible intellectual awareness of the learner. Students may judge that "I believe X as I had believed X before, but now I know why I believe X, and I also know that the certitude it exudes comes from my belief, not from natural, spiritual, unexamined sources that are other than or superior to my intellectual work and that of the other members of the LC." The power of beliefs now derives from the power of the believers' intellects and from the shared intellectual work of the LC.

For example, consider the old theological debate that reflects ambivalence about this qualitative transformation of belief, from belief in the ontological power of an external source to the subjective power of the believers' own internal assent. Whom does God love more, an innocent who never knows sin, or the sinner who does know it and repents? Who places higher in the stratification of heaven, the purely innocent or the purified sinner? Who is the greater being in the eyes of the Divine Judge, the Holy Innocents slaughtered as infants or Augustine, who knew sin well enough to pray for conversion and repentance, but not quite yet?

Clearly, these scenarios provide thought experiments, since the tradition out of which the quandaries derive also hold that all children of Eve know sin save two, Jesus and his mother, Mary. Presumably, each of us, after reaching the age of reason, fail to live up to our being in some metaphysical, moral or self-defined fault that took away our innocence through actions that meant something to us. Each of us can quickly recall such falls from grace—or is there a true innocent among us? Through self-interest alone, then, we are likely to opt for the full grace of the sinner who renounces sin, accepts grace, and reaffirms the salvific redemptive power of the Divine. Yet, the nagging doubt remains. The greatest saints often saw their failures rendering them into the most unworthy sinners, because of the rigorous edge of judgment they applied to themselves. So, too, intellectually repurified learners remain aware of the profound limits of what they, as individuals, know, as they reengage in the interactionally emergent power of the LC, in pursuit of socially efficacious and morally shared activities.

The inner ratio of saint-to-sinner that resonates within each of us mirrors the inner ratio of knower-to-ignorant, which is forever the pathos of humans, as essentially, though not empirically, rational animals. Each of us is an "animal rationale," as an "essence," at least in claim if not in practice, assuming that each of us is "*compos mentis*," or mentally competent. The vocation of a "professor" is to profess what the professor believes about the intellectual and communicative life of a community of learners. Rational intellect continually recalls us to this unending calling, and always in relationships with others. The inner ratios reflect the distinction between internal and external standards of truth and morality. In an LC, the filter of one's subjectivity is realized as an ongoing intersubjectivity, based on a prior social construction internalized and then attributed to be my individual and personal intellectual creation. This creation is, indeed, personal, but it is not in any literal sense merely individual.

Humans, in what they take to be knowledge of the world they know, inescapably fall into a "location fallacy": Because what I know is thought to "be in my mind," then it is mine in origin, meaning, and force. Wrong! Unless one chooses to be a reductive innatist—that is, holding the belief that each of us is born with a particular set of innate and totally individual truths—the fallacy is easy to see as a mote in the eye of the other, around the unseen beam in my own eye. Everything in my mind comes from outside somewhere, and if I can recognize the sources, I am better equipped to make it functionally my own, along with others for whom the meaning is valued, effectual, and implicated. LC dynamics aim for shared meanings that inform and underwrite continual and personal intellectual reassessment as a foundation for common life.

Meditation XXX: Historical Ruptures Illuminate Learning Community Pedagogy

Classical ways of seeing the world enacted and defined by human protagonists, as a prototype of traditional, conventional, and inherited ways of seeing, are based on an ontologization of history, on a fallacy of the past as cause, on a fallacy of the *apriori* as leading to tomorrow. Within institutionalizations of education, this ontologization of human pasts—as causal indicators of which human actions are efficacious and which goals are desirable—trumps the education of students' experience and not-yet conventional ways of seeing, and puts in its place an education into past ways of seeing and desiring action. In this form of education, knowledge and morality flow from the older to the younger. The flow from past to present to make futures informs and legitimates the "black box" model of education: institutions "transmit" knowledge from the head of the professor into the heads of students. In this context, read "head of the professor" to include all forms of packaging past knowledge, such as textbooks, classics, and older professors' validations of their way of seeing over that of the students.

Without developing an argument for the need to complement institutionalized education with experiential education, let me simply refer to what I take to be the defining feature of the dynamics driving this "postmodern" streaming society, namely, increasing rates of change in all interventions into nature, social structures, biographies, environments, and bodily interpretations and treatments. Rates of change are increasing at a speed and scope that belies the efficacy of learning how to respond from an ontologized past. The modern idea of cumulative knowledge that will enable humans to imagine a rational future and control nature, culture, society, and movements of peoples to fit into that *apriori-*

derived and authoritatively-imposed future is now seen as incomplete and inadequate, and, I suggest, dangerous.

In addition to emerging facilities in kinds and channels of knowledge and literacy, in which newer generations are more skilled, open, or experientially attuned, there is another dynamic effect that rapid social change occasions. Analysts speak of the "generation lag" as an extension of the idea of a "cultural lag" in understanding societal and institutional change. The succession of generations into positions of power and leadership typically puts people between 40 and 60 years of age in positions of political and policy power. Yet rapid social change suggests that these leaders and influentials grew up in a world that is significantly different from the world in which they govern. In this changed world, these leaders bring ways of seeing and acting, sets of values, logics of thought, and problem-solving that have a questionable fit with the problems of the day. People of power may not also be people of reflection, empirical openness, or interpretive flexibility. And when people of power emerge from a society of power, such as the United States is at the present moment, they bring both power to act and powerlessness to reflect on alternative meanings of their actions. Analysts have long commented on the nonintellectual, if not antiintellectual character of its leadership. The United States is, in part, a nation of shortterm doers with recurrent streaks of isolationism or unilateralism. LCP flies in the face of the pattern of gerontological leadership, just as it challenges the reductionist view that restricts knowledge to that which resides inside the heads of individuals, and especially individuals who rely on age, power, scarcity, and implicit punishment for control of learners' intellectual range and priorities.

Not all relevant ways of knowing are cumulative, and not all value priorities derive from preceding generations. These cautions apply especially in periods of rapid social change, which generate not only alternative interpretations of what it means to be authentically human and how one goes about living it, but also new and deeper modes of intervention into the contingencies of life itself, and of the conditions for sustaining that life, namely, issues of ultimate concern to humans and of proximate probabilities of surviving into future generations.

In summary, ruptures in societal dynamics and developments in technological knowhow—about never-before-possible deep interventions in environmental, life-sustaining, and inter-societal relationships—alter the premises upon which human evolution has functioned up until now. Hence arises the need for both supplementary kinds and dynamics of knowledge production and application, in the fullest sense of "knowledge," that is, value-informed and linked to inclusive justice, survival, and sustainability.

Humans, especially those who are most different from each other phenotypically and culturally, must come together in Learning Communities formed around issues with significant implications for all, and informed by an empirically-based approach to the first value of human species being, that is, just and peaceful survival amidst our circumstances. These kinds of Learning Communities are based on a shared commitment to empirical descriptions of the world as it is, and to a search for adequate causal understanding in the service of universal human values.

These kinds of learning emerge with a sense of play—that experience of a new and joyful self that emerges through fulfilling activities. This is the experience of an individual self who is a social individual playing with, nor merely parallel to and amidst, others. LCP, then, includes the creative moments of play, but it is and must be shared play. By shared play I do not mean a "game" with *apriori* rules, reductionist measurements, such as runs or points, and win-lose outcomes that define one participant as a successful winner and the other as a losing failure, and legitimates rewarding the winner and punishing the loser through loss of wealth, esteem, psychological well-being, or even one's life, as in as some traditional games played in distant cultures, such as among Roman gladiators and Aztec ball players.

Underlying the importance of play is the social-psychological axiom that we become what we play at. Learning and knowledge lived and generated through shared play contrasts with other kinds of learning and knowledge lived that is posited as serious and certain. Traditional religions give us a picture of a kind of knowing and learning that is "the serious life," as sociologist Émile Durkheim said of religions, and that is certain, as followers and proclaimers of faith insist. The seriousness of the paradoxical and, to some thinkers, oxymoronic category "religious knowledge" derives from its subject matter, a posited ultimate concern, and its validation—a revelation from Divinity itself. Of course, incarnated in the lives of believers and of their religious authorities, religious knowledge transforms group meanings and believers' identities into serious and certain social meanings that justify and motivate the most courageous and/or extreme actions, such as killing others, killing oneself, or, today, killing others by killing one's self.

I refer to this transformative power of a religious type of learning and knowledge as "eliminative identification," to indicate that my identity is universally and ultimately validated, such that any perceived threat to it may be countered by fundamental truths learned from authoritative teachers of the faith. Religious truth may motivate captors to behead a captive for failing to believe in the captor's God, and then to send the head to the captive's family members, to show the power of the captor's God.

The historical persistence, personal attraction, and social function of martyrs for handing on, recruiting, and reinforcing types of socio-cultural identities point to the personally and socially transformative power of an ultimate identity enacted in the service of the group's core values. A martyr embodies the ultimate hero identity, since he or she seals the group's collective identity by enacting it in the tragedy of sacrificing one's personal identity, one's life here on earth. Of course, in a transcendental religious belief system, that identity is regained in eternity, so that there is a utilitarian aspect to the tradeoff, akin to Pascal's classic reasoning about belief in God; or, in more contemporary parlance, the martyr may be minimizing his or her maximum loss—eternal damnation, earthly insignificance—while maximizing the maximum gain—eternal salvation.

The power of this mode of identity-formation and knowledge of a world makes an LCP impossible. Indeed, the kidnappers who beheaded their captives because they refused to believe in the captors' God, and then sent the heads to their relatives as a sign of God's judgment, were enacting the ultimacy of their divinely validated identity—an "eliminative identity," that is, the belief that my identity makes demands on me and on the other to conform to the sources of my identity, and if I or the other do not conform, then I or the other must be eliminated because God wills it, *Deus lo volt*!

LCP elicits opposite processes of identity-formation and validation of what is taken as knowledge of the world and of species futures. The love for self, each other, and learning, in an empirically-based and shared search for interpretations of the world around common universal issues, calls participants to what I think is a kind of "generative identity," that is, to processes that generate shared identities that include self and other while allowing each to retain distinctive aspects of inherited identities. Included in LCP's search for acceptance of the widest empirically-based truths relevant to the deepest shared issues is acceptance of the widest and most inclusive identities, which include both self and other. LCP, then, complements traditional religious and ideological pedagogies, by rendering them relevant to adherents' and believers' inherited identities, even as these same believers come to see the moral power of sharing the Earth's resources, freedom, and security with all other humans, regardless of their inherited identities. Thus, LCP generates a new, inclusive, and limited identity, as a member of the human species responsible each to each for its empirical survival, alongside whatever transcendent knowledge and identity believers live out otherwise. The eliminative identities of traditional religions and ideologies that lead to violence and conflict are synthesized within larger, timebound, earthly generative identities that mark all of us as members of the human species.

Meditation XXXI: Pessimism, Optimism, and Realism in a Learning Community

LC Pedagogy implies that worldly pessimism may be realism but psychological optimism is functional. More to the point of an LC is the assertion that optimism, contrary to the individualist heresy of our dominant culture, is a social emergent; and, more powerfully, that hope is a community virtue that emerges from our living together and the myths that sustain that common life. One of hope's everyday offspring is practical reasoning that links means to hoped- for ends and, to that degree, is operationally optimistic: If we do X, then we have a likelihood of achieving a desired Y.

Another, less appealing, offspring of the continua of hope-despair or pessimism-optimism is their illegitimate child, stress. Too often, the experience of scratching a hardworking and achieving student exposes a stressed and occasionally fearful young person. As a societal reflection, this professor's observations suggest that upon his arrival in the late 1960s, students were more middle class and upwardly mobile in the heady thrust of that time in the American Catholic community. By the time we reach the early twenty-first century, students are touched by postmodern pluralism, ephemerality, stress, and transitoriness. They are more upper class, with a future primarily circumscribed by the following: a struggle against falling, and striving to stay in the upper stratum of their family origin; downward generational and personal mobility and a social world that appears to "moving downward" as a species, with its habitat amidst profound and rapid global social and environmental dynamics; ever more destructive weapons of mass destruction; new biological threats that change the nature of sexual and interpersonal encounters; widespread local conflicts with global implications; environmental changes and causal shifts to paradoxical human interventions that both produce our preferred lifestyles and, in that very production, produce new threats to our lives; cyber-existence and the uncertain futures of artificial, robotic, and crossover life forms that may be aborning; and, finally, the heating up of our taken-for-granted social gatherings, by the hidden, violent identities of terrorists, especially those practicing and motivated by other-worldly sacred violence. Indeed, a professor must profess life in this stressful world in full support of the young, whose world it is much more than the professor's.

LCP is based on the assumption that to meet present human challenges by coping nobly with objective stressors and joyously with subjective stresses, interacting intellectuals share universal values in LCs to provide students an indispensible experience of efficacious social learning in the service of a hopeful future.

Meditation XXXII: Learning Community Pedagogy Looks toward Social Hope

Informing the vital dialectics of LCP is the dynamism for generating what I refer to as this-worldly social hope—an enveloping meaning that there are possible futures worthy of human effort, intelligence, and, indeed, sacrifice.

Paradox and pathos mark the experience and emergence of social hope. As a young person, I—and I believe most youngsters who experience a secure, if economically marginal. cultural childhood—took hope for granted. The future is the arena of possibilities, many of them desirable. Life is a "bowl of cherries," albeit with a few pits. As a middle-aged person, reflection on the precariousness of life led me to adopt the hard lemma that pessimism is realism. Life is a veil of tears. Living long enough to enter old age and rereading social-psychological writings about the meanings of a "future" unveiled a profound paradox that had escaped my earlier attention: Optimism is not only motivationally functional, it is a true vitalism. The future is an arena in which positive thinking motivates and sometimes begets better lives. Life is a beach, and I believe that tomorrow is another day.

As I now reflect on this succession of viewed futures, the third discovery is not a truth that replaces the second and reaffirms the first; nor is the third lemma an integration of the previous two; nor is it a truth that renders the previous two false. The third discovery that optimism is vitalism is a theological and philosophical teaching currently reiterated by biological reflection, and validated in part by empirical social-psychological research. Even everyday folk- psychology tells us that to think optimistically is good for motivating one's actions and getting out of bed in the morning. Scientific social-psychology, furthermore, tells that not only is optimistic thinking good for one's psychological health, but in measurable and, perhaps, surprising ways, for one's physical health as well.

A repeated scientific finding is that depressed people are living a kind of partial death, and optimistic people outperform and outlast those who are not so optimistic about the future that they believe is theirs. A plausibly important conclusion is that persons ought to think optimistically. Those who do not typically see the world as so rosy ought to learn how to tint it rosy, to put on action-oriented, rose-colored glasses, as it were.

Those of us who are parents would be well advised, since we wish the overall good of our daughters and sons in this life, to teach our children to think optimistically. And so, I believe, we should. Yet, true as I take that last sentence to be, it is not all of the story; indeed, it is not even the heart of the story. Here, as a cultural coda would have it, is the rest of the story. Optimism, as I have used the term above, and as I have interpreted the use of the term in the social-psychological and other literature, is a *formal* term. By "formal" I mean that there is no actional or experiential life-content included in the term. A person is "optimistic" about whatever in an imagined future gains the psychological payoff of good health, anticipated success, stress reduction, or whatever. A confident and competent hitman or terrorist, optimistic that his mark or victim will be fatally and clandestinely dispatched with a well placed car bomb, reaps the psychological benefits of optimistic thinking regardless of the morality of the actions.

Coda: Reversal of Efficacious Knowledge in a Learning Community: From Pedagogy to Gerogogy

Classical knowledge flow is mirrored in the metaphors informing the etymology of the names attached to teaching/learning: Consider the Greek roots in "pedagogy" and Latin roots in "education." From the Greeks we find reflections of the gendered access to learning: "*Ped*" comes from the Greek word for boy, and "*gogy*" from the word indicating rearing or training. And so it was for most of history until this century; and the gendered access to learning is still an obstacle to the development of women in many cultural contexts. Indeed, playing with Greek roots, I would like to think in terms of "anthropogogy," except for its unwieldiness. That is, I seek a term that applies to all humans, "anthropoi," regardless of gender, as the goals, means, and potential for universal human development and maximization of the knowledge and sharing needed to sustain ourselves as a species through gender-free learning. It is not education of the boy or the man—a collective noun with its built-in gender ambiguity—but of the human, of the person.

In addition to gendered access, there is the classical, and still presumed, aged access: The older rear and instruct the younger. And this, of course, is inescapable for the first years of development. Yet changes are recently seen in the inherited structure of aged access to learning, at least that which is based on the transmission of knowledge from the older to the younger. Indeed, in realms of cyberlearning and communications, as well as discoveries in the basic sciences and mathematics, aged access is being restructured in nontraditional ways. In some contexts, we may speak of "gerogogy" or, as entertainment would have it, "Bringing up Father."

The pictures and faded metaphors carried in the Latin roots that nuance our thinking about teaching/learning inform the meanings of "education." It also refers to rearing and training by another who "leads" (ducere) the learner away from ignorance. Yet it carries a promising, additional penumbra of meanings from the basic metaphor of eliciting or bringing to life or efficaciousness that which is latent or potential in the other. By analogy with induction and deduction, whereby we arrive at new understanding by moving from arrays of empirical happenings or from logical links among interrelated propositions, so we arrive at new understandings of self, other, and world by processes of "education." I prefer this metaphor and its family of related ideas to that of pedagogy. Education appeals to that which is potentially universal in all members of the human species, such as survival, solidarity, hope, and compassion. I think of these as presocial potentials in our species being, potentials that LCP elicits and fulfills as a function of a social being learning socially.

www.ingramcontent.com/pod-product-compliance
Lightning Source LLC
Chambersburg PA
CBHW021109080526
44587CB00010B/451